OVER AND BACK IN CONNEMARA

by

Amy Laidlaw
Heather Welsh

Published by

Amy Laidlaw
Heather Welsh

Copyright © 2000

No part of this book may be reproduced, stored
in a retrieval system, or transmitted in any form,
or by any means electronic, mechanical, photocopying,
recording or otherwise without the prior consent of the
Publishers and the Copyright holders.

Printed and bound by
The College Press,
a division of the University of Hull

ISBN 0 9539094 09

INTRODUCTION

Almost one hundred years after the publication (W.H. Allen & Co. Ltd. 1893) of Sommerville and Ross's classic 'Through Connemara in a Governess cart' two early retired secretaries record their decision to sell up in Dublin and set off for Connemara. The events experienced by these women almost a century apart reflect the similarities and the differences of social conditions in rural Ireland.

The new venture of a personalised guest house promised the enjoyment of meeting the local people, getting to know their customs and heritage and welcoming visitors from all parts of the world.

The authors recall the vicissitudes of gardening in the tree-less boulder-strewn land, the coralling of Connemara ponies and sympathising with rabbit hunters on the Golf Course. Mysterious happenings on the Bog Road are related in hushed tones !

List of Contents

Quotation . . . .
Changing Course 7
Decision Time 8-9
Property 10-13
The Moving In 15-17
Tomorrow Never Comes - But It Did 25-27
The First Christmas 28-31
Ater Christmas 32-37
'It Always Rain in the West' - Not So 32-37
Ready for Business 38-40
The First Paying Guests 41-42
The Garden - Not of Eden Because No
  Apple Trees : No Trees 43-50
Hands Across the Sea 51-53
If I Could Talk to the Animals and They
  Could Talk to Me 54-61
Connemara Good Samaritans 62-66
Let There Be Light 67-70
Sleeping Rough 71-72
I Must Go to the Sea Again 73-75
Religious Observances 76-79
Visitors 80-84
The Landladies' Holiday 85-92
Conversation Pieces 93-101
Tthe Long Arm of Coincidence 102-104
More Than Guest Housing - The Tourist Bit 105-113
The School Around the Corner 114-116
Palmistry - Reading the Local Map 117-121
Getting to Know the ICA 122-129
Tthe Parting of the Ways 130-131
Over the Back To Connemara - June 1995 132-135

Illustrations by Phebe Kinghorn

' Ireland is a place where the inevitable never happens and the unexpected always occurs. '

Sir John Pentland Mahaffy
1839 - 1919

CHANGING COURSE

Redundancy, early retirement, call it what you will, can be a traumatic experience. On the other hand it can provide opportunity and challenge as we proved when we gave up city life in Dublin and embarked on an incident and action-packed new 'career' in the west of Ireland from 1980.

We now live in the U.K. - Amy in Edinburgh, Scotland, and Heather in Hull, England, meeting regularly when our talk centres on the ten years we spent in Brandyburn Cottage, Ballyconneely, Co. Galway.

This is a story we have been urged to tell by our many friends in Ireland and beyond - friends old and new whom we helped to enjoy that magical place called Connemara.

If you do not know of it, take your map of Ireland, draw a line due west from Dublin reaching the furthermost coast of County Galway, find Ballyconneely six miles south of Clifden.

Next stop across the Atlantic Ocean is Boston and there are millions of Irish emigrants who wistfully turn their eyes eastwards towards the Emerald Isle.

No doubt many of our friends will recognise themselves in this story for they joined in listening to our enthusiasm for the new life and the many tales we told against ourselves.

We now look back on our treasure trove of memories of life in Connemara but before we continue, we gratefully acknowledge the tremendous kindness of the local people of Ballyconneely who accepted two Scotswomen and indulged us in our innocence and indeed ignorance of rural ways.

DECISION TIME

Many people have decided on their future during a walk on the East Pier Dun Laoghaire, near Dublin, to the tinkling of the tackle on the yachts moored there.

Taking deep breaths of the ozone one glorious Sunday morning we were aware of an unusual seaside sound which appeared to accompany the tinkling notes of the tackle. Across the stillness of the harbour came the clear notes of a musical instrument playing Mozart. Looking over the sea wall, we saw a young man sitting down below on the huge rocks fair hair atop his blue sweatshirt silhouetted against the sky blissfully enjoying playing a clarinet. We left him to his solitude, his clarinet glinting in the sunlight. Continuing our stroll along the pier we heard in the distance the haunting strains of 'Stranger on the Shore' - very appropriate to the situation.

During these early Sunday morning walks our talk ranged far and wide, bouncing ideas off each other, holiday notions, the future and, more recently the conversation drew to our imminent early retirement.

'It is lovely and calm this morning - going to be a warm day.'

'Mmmm, yes. It must be nice to live at the seaside. Wonder if it feels like one long holiday? You know, I always had a notion, well a dream really, of owning a small country hotel close to the sea.'

'Why didn't you?'

'The opportunity wasn't there and anyway the Prize Bond Draw didn't oblige.'

'Yes, looking at Dun Laoghaire today it's an enticing thought and I must admit I have often thought of the attraction of a small hotel.'

'Why didn't you go for it?'

'The opportunity wasn't there and anyway the Prize Bond didn't oblige!! '

'Have you decided what you will do in early retirement?' 'No - not yet.'

'How about being a seaside landlady?'

'Financially I couldn't do it on my own. How about you? Any more ideas?'

'I had thought about an old fashioned teashop with home baking, but when I weighed up the pros and cons, there were too many cons! I still hanker after the Guest House / Hotel idea. Do you fancy it? What about County Galway? There would surely be room for another Guest House....'

The idea of a Guest House coming more into focus through talking of it, we went along to Bord Failte, the Irish Tourist Board, and discussed the viability of such a venture in the Galway area.

We had spent our working lives in the secretarial field, jobs which had given lots of fulfilment and the opportunity to enjoy organisation, travel, social entertaining, conference work, and, in our leisure time, cooking, handcrafts and an interest in the arts.

Now was the time to step forward to a new life which meant selling the two houses in Dublin and investing our limited capital in the idea of a small, personalised Guest House.

In good cowboy stories the advice was given 'Go West young man' and so we metaphorically hitched up our covered wagon and, as pioneers in days of old, went speculating for property in County Galway, an area we had both come to love.

PROPERTY

Our specification was for a house all on one level, if possible, not too big and not too small, in a tourist area where we could enjoy the countryside out of season. Obtaining brochures of possible properties we took a weekend trip, making our base in Oughterard. Staying in a Guest House we had visited before, we looked at it now with a new eye, not merely as a guest but visualising what went on behind the scenes from a business point of view.

We had property to view in Oughterard and, with the Agent, called there in the evening. Going round the house we made a discovery about each other - Amy knocked on walls and Heather had an obsession about three-pin flat electric plugs. We were very impressed about the other's apparent vast knowledge of building and electricity which was quite unfounded as we discovered at our later post mortem of our first viewing of property. We hoped we had given the Agent an impression of our knowledge of building construction. At first sight the house did not appeal to us - too far off the main road and not large enough for a Guest House. There was too much land requiring continual attention and a chalet style fishing lodge complete with boat house amounted altogether to more than what we required, especially when we discovered a pets' cemetery in the grounds!

First one scored off the list.

Next stop was Leenane, north of Clifden. This time it was a Guest House but, although in a lovely position, it was awkward to reach – both by foot as there were too many steps up to the door and, by car, a steep gradient - pity the nervous driver faced with a 1 in 8 slope! The house itself had an upstairs and downstairs and as we were unlikely to have a Hudson, First Parlour Maid and Tweenie as staff, that property was also a large 'NO' for us.

Leenane is a beautiful little village at the head of Killary Harbour which is a replica of a Norwegian fjord. The area was later to be used in the film 'The Field' from the book written by the Irish writer, John B. Keane, many local inhabitants taking part in the film.

It was time to hitch up the wagon again and head south, this time taking the road by Cashel to Roundstone, a village on the coast and an area much favoured by artists. The property we were to view was by the sea and the instructions from the House Agent, some fifty miles distant, was to collect the key from an adjacent cottage.This was our first introduction to the wonderful casual pace of life in the West. As we drew up we decided the house didn't look 'vacant', nor was it. Formerly owned for some years by a well-known author, it now transpired that it was the property of a favourite pop-star. Amy's credit rating soared to the heavens when later our friends' teenage families discovered she had actually spoken to this idol. However, number three property was not for us. It wouldn't have suited our purpose.

The beautiful coastal road from Roundstone took us to Ballyconneely. That day the sun was shining in a clear blue sky, the sea was sparkling and the sandy beaches were waiting in readiness for the next tide to come in and the visitors to swim in the clear, totally unpolluted water. This is one of the great joys of Connemara and we realised why the road from Roundstone to Ballyconneely is noted in the AA Gazetteer as the Brandy and Soda Road because of its exhilarating air !

The next brochure from the House Agent indicated a property one mile from this road at Ballyconneely village. Our goal came into view, expectations were rising.

The red-roofed cottage, then known as the Red Cottage, had turf smoke spiralling from its chimneys and the scented air promised well. It was set back a little from the road with no enclosing fences or wall to the front. Along its eighty foot length the ground had been left free to accommodate parked cars or as a pull-in for passing traffic.

We studied the cottage which was a long low building, and saw a small side porch. The first window to the front appeared to be a dining room. Next along was a low-set half-door, a split door whose purpose is to let in air and light when the top half is opened, the bottom half being kept closed against inquisitive animals. From articles on the sills of the next two windows it was evident that this was the kitchen. Further on, the windows indicated a sitting room. This then was the front elevation of the house with its doors and window frames painted red to match the roof.

The cottage had character; was not a 'beauty', in fact at the front it was a bit strait-laced but going round to the back the character took over.

Announcing our arrival we were invited inside. Our initial first impression outside of a very small cottage proved deceptive when we entered via the porch and stepped into a long corridor with doors on either side, white painted walls broken by wrought iron coach lamps.

A small bedroom had a window on to the entrance porch which sported a ship's navigation lamp. Next came the dining room with its timbered beams and a fireplace of pebbles honed to rounded smoothness by countless tides. Who in the past had gone pebble hunting to select the right shades and colour?

The square kitchen was a good size with cupboards and presses lining the walls. Cooking was by a five-burner bottled gas stove with cylinder within and an oven; as a back-up there was a small electric cooker. A large rough hewn stone fireplace glowed with a turf fire.

The sitting room with its two large windows facing the road also had one to the west side. It was a large bright room with yet another stone fireplace sending wisps of smoke up the wide chimney.

Turning from our inspection of these rooms we viewed four bedrooms and from another shorter corridor two further bedrooms, all facing south. On the east elevation of the house was an eighth bedroom and, of course, they were all on one level.

Because of some extensions having been built at the back of the cottage, two possible patio areas were apparent which with planting would lend attraction.

With the sun streaming in on every side it was a pleasant, lived-in house with potential for our purpose. Our visit was measuring up quite well to what we had in mind. The views at the rear drew eyes across unspoiled terrain of boulder-strewn land to the sparkling sea beyond. We obtained permission to take photographs inside and out so that we could better remember what we had seen.

Having made enquiries about utilities, central heating system, supplies of turf, availability of service engineers and tradesmen who might be necessary in the future, we thanked the owners for their courtesy and hospitality and made our way to the Coral Strand, which would be a favourite stopping place in the future.

Even discounting the amusing antics of the seagulls who 'dive-bombed' us and our potato crisps which 'went with the wind', we don't think we enjoyed the picnic lunch we had brought for there was so much to discuss.

Keeping up a barrage of questions and possible answers we considered – What could the Red Cottage do for us? What would be necessary to make it 'our own' if we decided it was suitable for our purpose?

Yes, we considered it was a property two women could cope with as we wished to do everything ourselves.

Yes, we could do most of the annual maintenance required by a one-level white painted cottage, and yes, we could easily wash the many windows from a standing start both inside and out, even though we are only five feet plus.

Renovations would be required. Window frames could be changed, toilet and bathroom facilities improved, the property rewired for electricity to latest EC standard. Yes, a lot would be necessary.

Yes, we agreed we had the energy and incentive for the creation of our personalised Guest House.

Mindful of the time when full retirement would beckon, long term plans for that were borne in mind, but the challege was here and now. We returned to Oughterard where we were staying for the weekend and decided to sleep on everything we had seen and discussed and ponder on the ramifications if we were to make a decision.

Next day came further analysis. What would be required for the house itself? What could **we** do with the rough land enclosed in its drystone walls which would be ours? Could **we** ever tame it, grow flowers and vegetables: in other words, make a garden against the elements? There were paths at the back of the house. For a start we'd have to plod in wellies into the rough ridgy ground to hang our washing. Paths would be one of the early necessities.

Notebooks and pens worked overtime as we figures and drafted cost sheets, thought of time-scales, highlighted the good points and made sure snags had been considered.

After another visit to the Cottage, the legalities were set in motion for the property to become ours.

Following this, enquiries were made from friends who had cottages in the area as to recommendations of local contractors. We made our choice, specified our requirements, time scale and agreed costs.

All this time, Heather's mother, Chris-Ann aged 90, was one of the trio of pioneering women going West. She took a lively interest in everything and enjoyed her new life there till her death in 1982.

The time had come to tell our friends. Heather and her mother had come to Ireland in 1954 and Amy in 1971. After such a number of years we each had many friends. Most of the reaction from them after the initial shock was 'we were very brave' : 'we were mad ' : 'it always rained over there'. Perhaps we were 'brave' and 'mad' but in life sometimes we have to prove something to ourselves. We regarded it as a new direction in our lives, determined to try it and equally determined to make it work to the best of our abilities.

THE MOVING IN

After farewell parties, advice, good wishes and gifts from our friends, the day came when our 'moving experience' began, 11 November 1980. The furniture was collected by the removers from Heather's house in Terenure and after a 'phone call to Amy alerting her of the van's expected arrival in Dundrum, Heather and Chris-Ann headed off to Oughterard, complete with the trailer filled with favourite plants.

At Amy's in Dundrum, the furniture was packed into the van to bursting point. Finally, turning the key in the door and with a last look around the house which had been her home for ten years, Amy headed off for the Hotel in Oughterard to meet up with Heather and her mother. After a couple of 'jars', a good traditional Irish expression for a drink, to toast the success of the venture we gratefully fell into comfortable beds. For all of us it had been a journey of mixed feelings of nostalgia and excitement.

The following morning was a crisp frosty sunny day and after a hearty Irish breakfast we harnessed the horse power of the two cars for the second leg of the journey. Driving along the last 38 miles we appreciated the majesty of the Twelve Pins range of mountains, the deep blue of the many lochs and the rich brown turf. Blue smoke lazily rising from folds in the land were, at times, the only indication of habitation, and we marvelled at the families who lived in this beautiful, but wild, countryside.

The furniture van had travelled from Dublin to Galway where it stayed overnight completing the last fifty miles in the morning. We managed to arrive before them and the great unloading commenced. The Red Cottage having been a Guest House already had beds in every room and we had a further eight. Talk about putting quarts into pint pots ! It was the same situation in the dining room and sitting room where we seemed to be surrounded by furniture as if it was going to rise and take over.

The previous owners, John and Rita, had kindly left a very welcoming turf fire smouldering in the kitchen grate and soon we had a cheerful blaze.

Just as the last of our possessions had been taken into the house, it started to rain and by the end of the day a westerly gale was blowing. It had been a real Vivaldi experience - all four seasons in one day.

By the following morning the storm had blown over : the winter sunshine was in place and all was well with the world. Stepping out briefly into the rain-washed landscape we heard for the first time the sounds around us. Loch Aesard, where our water supply came from, was across the road and from there came bird calls - an argument between seagulls and, nearer, the impatient chatter of stonechats. Cattle and sheep joined the chorus, not to mention a pair of donkeys enjoying a joke and the cry of a fox. As the days went by we realised we had much to learn in identifying sounds with animals.

Returning to the kitchen the fire needed our attention. A box of dried turf sat on the hearth and with a gentle raking a couple of sods were put on endways to catch in the embers. In true pioneering spirit, the next consideration was attending to the inner (wo)man and soon the kettle was boiling, the porridge was simmering and we were ready to tackle the first day of our new life.

We determined to be as self-sufficient as possible and do all the jobs that a man might be expected to take care of. Coming from city life with the convenience of all mod cons an early priority was to establish how the central heating system worked. It was soon discovered that the oil-fired system of radiators throughout the property brought its own problems. A very temperamental boiler which was housed in an out-building had us running in and out to give it a 'kick-start', quite literally on occasions for at times it seemed to be four parts temper and six parts mental. It would have to be replaced in time.

Amy was the one who undertook to deal with the boiler when it went on the blink and one dark night not long after our moving in she had to go to the boiler house. After the kick-start method had proved successful, the boiler house light switched off, she returned to the house. At this time there was neither light nor proper path round the back of the house so stumbling along with a torch you can imagine her shocked surprise to come face to face with a large black cow. Which of them got the bigger fright!

Encouraging the boiler and coaxing the turf fire were only two of the new tricks the old dogs - we can't use the correct word - had to learn and there were many more to come. Euphoria was being challenged.

Having been in touch with the local electrical contractor from Clifden, Jackie Ward, and building contractor from Ballyconneely, Gerry McCann, on a previous visit, we arranged for both of them to come after we moved in for an on-site discussion regarding the work to be undertaken. The main project was re-wiring to comply with EC Regulations and as the cottage was stone it meant the builders bring in a jack hammer to channel the walls and floors for electric cable ducting. After the grand inspection tour had been made and coffee taken, they departed with the remark, 'We'll go and have a consultation'.

When we had been telling our friends in Dublin of our planned 'change of life' we were regaled with dire stories of time and dates of work to be done which appeared to be not very important to contractors. So when they said 'We'll go and have a consultation' we concluded our worst fears were going to happen - 'putting the job on the long finger'. It was a big job, Christmas was coming, and an Easter opening was planned. That night we sat around the ould turf fire in the kitchen with our spirits rather low, yet trying to be cheerful, saying sentences which began with 'perhaps' .... and 'maybe' ....

Later in the evening someone knocked at the door. 'Who could this be?' we asked each other.

On opening the door, the six-foot Gerry McCann folded into the kitchen and breezily told us, 'We'll be in first thing tomorrow morning to start the job. See ye. Bye'. Folding up again he shot out the doorway.

Had it really happened? Had this young giant, who turned out to be a neighbour and latterly our mentor, actually said they would start tomorrow?

We went off to bed feeling more cheerful and mentally ready for the work to start in the morning.

TOMORROW NEVER COMES - BUT IT DID

Promptly at nine o'clock Gerry, with his brother Joe, another six footer, Martin and Terence came in the kitchen door, pulling off coats as they did so, saying, 'Morning Amy, Morning Mrs. Welsh, Morning Heather'. They didn't stop, just walked on and out into the long hall-way where we could hear instructions being rapped out about carpet and furniture, etc. Ten minutes later we were startled by the sound of a heavy drill, and running into the hall found the noise came from the sitting room. Amidst a rising cloud of concrete dust we saw the furniture including the piano, had been pulled into the centre of the room and the carpet dragged over from the walls to cover it all. It looked like a rugged island in a grey misty sea. The hall carpet had also been lifted and put away in the large concrete shed which we liked to think of as our utility room. It sounded so much better! It was fortunate that new carpets throughout the cottage were planned.

During the renovations we camped in and out of every one of the eight bedrooms until each in turn was required for attention by the heavy drill of Gerry and Pete, the electrician. Pete, a Dorset man, had come to the area on holiday some years before, liked it so much and had just never left. All the activity was accompanied by animated chatter among 'the fellas', as we had come to know them. Such conversations we found confusing and alarming for we hadn't yet become attuned to the high pitched local accent, plus the Dorset one, and many times we questioned if all was well or had unexpected problems arisen, only to be told, 'Ah, no, no, no, no'.

During this time we ourselves had become very proficient at moving beds and mattresses from one room to the other, but not without problems, especially at the tight corners in the corridor. The main difficulty was that we dissolved into helpless fits of laughter. Between all this scene shifting and gentle hysteria, we kept 'the fellas' going with coffee and biscuits, even managing a mini celebration for Martin's twenty-first birthday, albeit a wee cake with lit candle and a packet of fags! The kitchen worktop was a continual battle area of mugs, milk, boiling kettles and coffee, not forgetting an over-flowing ash tray.

Most days we escaped from the hustle and bustle and took the oppor-tunity to explore the countryside more closely letting the lads get on with their mayhem. Some days when we returned, it looked as though the house was on fire, but it was just the concrete dust billowing from the open windows. After the fellas had gone home for the day we had to clear away their canteen, brush the quarry tile kitchen floor, then wash the pans and dishes we were going to use before we could even begin to prepare our evening meal. The dust was just everywhere.

As we had established a good rapport with Gerry, our mentor, it be-came the usual thing when something puzzled us to 'put it on the Gerry list'. This was a clipboard pinned up in the kitchen and became a focal point of reference. Indeed Gerry, as he tumbled through the half door each morning, would glance at our cryptic notes. When we had expanded on them he would have a slight smile on his face as he enlightened us. He and his colleagues came to know the extent of our innocence and indeed ignorance, and we are quite sure they discreetly conveyed to the neighbourhood that the newcomers were no threat to the local community!

Previously we had learned that even before taking over the property word had gone around Ballyconneely as to who we were and what our background had been - 'businesswomen - no experience in guesthousing - and not even Irish ! How could they possibly cope?'

The puncture repair was an item on the Gerry list. Not having a garage, the cars were parked at the front of the house and going out one morning Amy discovered a rear tyre had a puncture, and no evident local garage. Gerry and Joe quickly changed the wheel and directed us to Gerry O'Malley's garage at Aillebrack to have the puncture repaired. We followed their instructions which took us along a winding road, the sides of which were further narrowed by sand drifts. Cresting the brow of a small hill, the road stopped short and we faced a bay with sea water at high tide. On the other bank was a cottage, a car, children's toys on the grass and a road running away from the sea. We reversed the car with difficulty, convinced we had gone the wrong way but, no, in five minutes we enquired at a house and a man pointed across the land. He gave the same directions, saying, 'Gerry's garage is just over there'.

We wailed, 'But we've just come from there - it's all sea and no way across'.

He smiled encouragingly, 'Sure you'll be all right'.

Playing safe, we chickened out and took the offending wheel the eight miles to Clifden for repair. When we returned home and told Gerry and Joe of our problem they fell about laughing.

A few weeks later the said Gerry O'Malley had collected Heather's car and taken it for a minor repair, saying he would return it if he could get a lift home. When Gerry arrived, Heather craftily suggested he keep in the driving seat : she would then find out the proper way to his garage. Coming to our 'Waterloo' it was low tide and Heather said to Gerry, 'Oh, so that's what we should have done, gone around in a sweeping bend'.

He was laughing when he replied, 'Yes, we all heard of your efforts a week or two ago. At least you were lucky. A local man who knew the area very well was driving his little new van and approaching the bay thought he could beat the incoming waves. He started across but didn't have enough power, the waves lapped in the open windows and he had to scramble free'. Gerry continued, 'The shiny new vehicle had to be towed out by tractor'.

At least we had been spared such indignity.

In the evenings we sat in the kitchen in the gathering December darkness reflecting on our new life in the West, and particularly Ballyconneely, the village which is a sprawling area so the quite large population is widely scattered. Like so many other Irish villages, it has its Post Office with shop attached, the family of the post mistress running this well-stocked thriving business. Just over the boundary wall are the grounds of the local Catholic Church, an attractive white building reminiscent of Spanish architecture, and beyond is the Community Hall built by the local inhabitants in 1958.

Across from the Church is Keogh's Pub, a well-known landmark and something of a social centre for the villagers, largely due no doubt to Mrs. Keogh, the owner, and her family. The other part of the building is taken up by their Supermarket. Again another thriving business.

Outside Keogh's is the rendezvous point once a week for the Garda (police) car for those who 'sign on' to obtain State benefit. There is very little regular employment in the area, most of the men work their land, tend a few cattle and cut turf for the house.

The nearest branch of the Bank of Ireland was Clifden, but many of the villages throughout Connemara are serviced by a travelling bank. On Friday mornings at two locations in Ballyconneely its arrival is eagerly awaited. We were impressed by the courtesy and unwritten understanding by local people that only one person at a time entered, ensuring teller / customer confidentiality.

Another outstanding feature in the village which intrigued us when we first arrived were two Notices on a triangular piece of land at a road junction. One proclaimed 'No Dumping. By Order of Galway County Council' and alongside in five languages the second stated what time rubbish was to be dumped ! There were frequently near-traffic jams as tourists jockeyed for position to photograph this apparent contradiction.

There was no refuse collection at houses, but once a week rubbish could be taken to this triangular plot of land at the stated time and it was then removed to a dump close to Galway city.

One morning whilst 'dumping' , Heather noticed the local Curate, Father Seery, coming towards her, complete with camera. Introducing himself, he explained he was in touch with Galway County Council to stop the present arrangement and introduce a new system of collection at houses or, where necessary, at narrow roadends, and to open up a landfill site in the hills at the back of Clifden. His camera was to show the County Council the volume of rubbish which was presently left in the centre of Ballyconneely. As his house was on the land adjacent it was not a very hygienic situation for him - seagulls and animals liked to rummage, consequently bursting bags and adding to the health hazard. Father Seery's good intentions were to be successful in due course and were much appreciated by everyone in the new collection area.

Later we were to discover that at the beginning of winter when the strong winds and high seas blew in from the Atlantic, a certain stretch of the road at the end of a sea inlet suddenly started to sport plastic bunting on the barbed wire fencing. This came from rubbish dumped off shore and also further out at sea. If one was of an enquiring mind it was possible to learn by reading the labels on the bottles and cans where the commodity had originated. The plastic bunting gradually disintegrated and by springtime, tall grasses and wild flowers had regained the initiative.

Sitting in the kitchen in our nightly discussions we spoke of what was to us something of a culture shock. Imagine, in the 1980s a 'phone service restricted to the hours of eight a.m. until ten p.m. during weekdays, even less on Sundays and yet paying the rental as for a full service. Too bad if anyone needed to make an urgent telephone call in the night time hours, in which case it would be necessary to travel to the public kiosk in the village which was linked directly to Clifden Exchange. Ballyconneely's manual Exchange operated from the local Post Office.

The personal involvement of the postmistress was a blessing in disguise for, knowing all the local people, she had to deal with many calls including international ones for them and for relatives abroad. Good news hopefully, but on occasion tragic messages were sensitively conveyed. The telephone is a worldwide lifeline.

Some years later while Amy was on holiday Heather broke her ankle and was hobbling around the house slowly so she asked the Post Office to plug in any calls and she would answer as fast as she could. A caller from Dublin was impressed to be told to hold on as the lady had broken her ankle. There are definite advantages in living in a country area with only a manual telephone service: we were quite sorry when the service became automatic. We certainly benefited from the personal and pleasant co-operation of our local postmistress.

During this period of house renovation it was total exhaustion by the end of the working day and total relaxation in the evenings, but time was moving on and so was the work.

The kitchen was the last bastion to be attacked and at this point it was no longer possible for us to live with the contractors and they to work round us so we had to bail out for three days to let them complete the extra wiring. In a way it was a relief for us to stay in Galway in the comfort of a small hotel when we could enjoy peace and quiet to think and plan ahead.

All this massive house upheaval lasted to near Christmas by which time we had allocated the beds to the rooms and the furniture for the dining and sitting rooms. Our new electric wall-mounted oven was in place ready for the turkey to be cooked.

The weeks since our arrival had been like living on a building site. We had worn an unofficial uniform of trousers and sweaters which were quite literally worn out. Amy said her beautiful purple mohair sweater reminded her of the Fairy Flag in Dunvegan Castle in Skye, but not having such an illustrious history the sweater went out with the rest of the rubbish.

When the workmen had stopped for their Christmas/New Year break our nesting instincts took over. We tidied the sitting room, relaying the old carpet and piled the mountain of unopened black plastic sacks and cardboard boxes to one end. With favourite pieces of furniture, pictures, lamps and ornaments we created a haven of almost normality around the fireplace.

Sitting in this relative comfort in the evenings we couldn't help but chuckle over the forthcoming Christmas turkey and scenes in Galway which we had witnessed.

The previous owner of the cottage, Rita, had given her small flock of hens to Mary Jo, a neighbour. We came to know Mary Jo quite well during her forays into our garden to collect the hens which kept coming back to familiar ground thinking they were homing pigeons.

Knowing Mary Jo also had turkeys we decided to have what to us would be a really fresh home grown bird - one which we had seen scrabbling around her house. Never backward at coming forward, Amy asked if we could order and though she and Mary Jo didn't exactly spit on their hands in traditional manner of striking a bargain, an amicable agreement was reached.

One day when Mary Jo was rounding up her hens, to our surprise she asked did we wish the bird dead or alive. Apparently some people prefer to take live turkeys home, fatten them up and then do the dastardly deed for their Christmas dinner.

Our past experience of turkeys was being handed over the butcher's counter a very dead bird, beautifully dressed ready for the oven !

A few days later this dead/alive turkey syndrome came home to roost when we were in a pub in Galway. Heather returned from placing the food order clutching two glasses of Bristol Cream.

'You'll never believe this. There's a live turkey in the next booth', said Amy. 'Look over'.

Sure enough, in a wicker basket at the feet of an elderly couple sat the proud turkey, neck and head emerging from the cloth cover of the basket and enjoying its scrutiny of the customers, the neck and head twisting hither and thither.

No one else seemed the least bit perturbed. We realised it was market day and no doubt the couple had come into town to choose their live bird from a visiting breeder who, in the market square, paraded his flock from his van.

We supposed the turkey and its new owners would go home by bus but did the turkey ever get a drink in the pub to sustain its travel ?

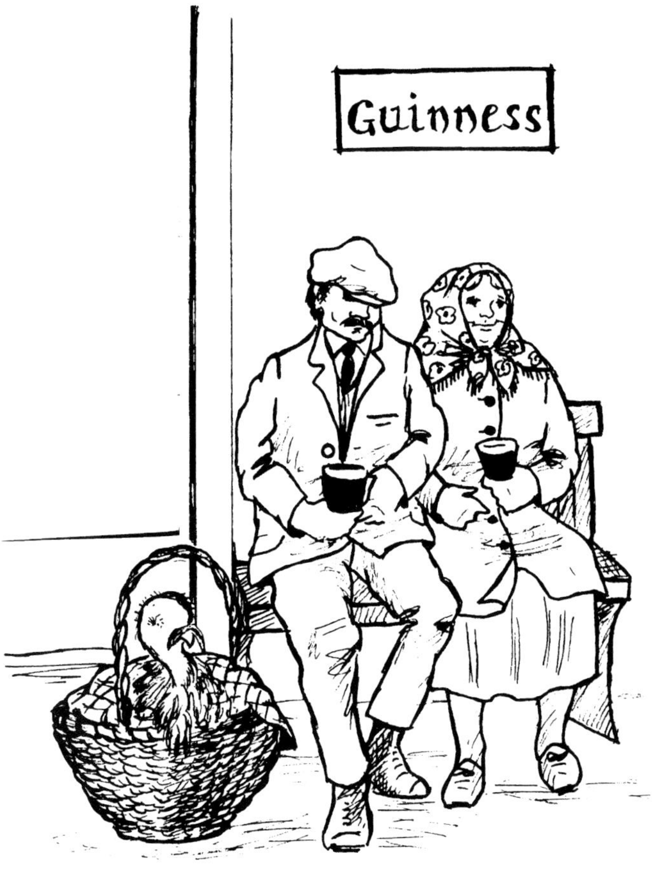
Guinness

THE FIRST CHRISTMAS

It was a lovely morning. The sun was shining and a steady stream of parishioners on foot, bicycle, car and even horseback passed on the way to attend Mass in the village.

After the local people had become used to the new owners of the house, which they had known as the Red Cottage and was now called Brandyburn Cottage, they would acknowledge us in passing. This was so on Christmas Day although they knew, as villagers always learn quickly of newcomers, that we were not of their faith: we had increased the very small number of Protestants in the area.

We had anticipated that our first Christmas in the west would be very different from those in the past. We received many cards and gifts but had very little space to display them. There were no parties with our friends from Dublin to look forward to: no visits to exchange gifts: no meeting friends in Bewley's Coffee House, nor going to favourite haunts for a 'Christmas jar'. We just accepted that our old life-style had changed and a new one was evolving.

Preparations for our first Christmas in Connemara were under way. We would have our Christmas lunch in the kitchen in the middle of the day and to this end remembered the Delia Smith cookery lessons we had watched on TV, dredged up all the teaching by our mothers and aunties in days gone by and plastered the turkey with butter, giving it an overcoat of fatty bacon. How our digestive juices were running, never mind the turkey's juices and it hadn't even been put in our shining new oven. Timing it just right, 'the beast' slid gracefully into the large oven, rather like an elegant large ship being launched into the depths of the sea for the very first time. Oh, but it was going to be a grand feast like no other. After an hour or so we realised one thing was missing - the enticing aroma of cooking. It was a large bird, but it should have been teasing our taste buds by this time. Panic ! The cooker wasn't working. It was barely warm. We checked all our newly installed system of trip switches but soon found that the fault was not in the house, so therefore out of our control.

After going to the village and leaving a message on the answering service at the Electricity Company, plan B came into operation, so we lit the bottled gas cooker, which we had inherited with the house and transferred the turkey. We discovered, to our dismay, that the oven pressure was very low in comparison to an electric cooker so we were left anticipating our highly prized, very dead turkey with all the trimmings for much longer than intended. We were ready for Christmas Day but would the turkey ever be ready ?

Here we were, the three of us, all dressed up and nowhere to go and nothing to eat sitting around the kitchen fireplace.

'Hey, Amy, it's good to see you out of that purple mohair sweater at last,' said Heather, 'though you're keeping to the kitchen theme by wearing your velvet pinafore dress !'

Chris-Ann and Amy laughed at this terrible joke and Amy said, 'Well I must say your string of pearls add a touch of style to the kitchen along with your high heels ! When did you last wear those?'

Before Heather could reply, Chris-Ann chipped in, 'When she last ran after a double decker bus and got stuck in a crack in the pavement!'

What a picture - just sitting there in the fire glow patiently waiting for the feast. It vividly brought back to us a verse from an old Scottish song. Our few sherries had loosened the tension and the tongues, and we sang first quietly and then louder with great feeling -

> By the light o' the peat fire flame
> Light for love, for lilt, for laughter
> By the light o' the peat fire flame
> The light the hill folk yearn for.

And so it was that we at last had our first Christmas Dinner in Brandyburn Cottage by candlelight and, at last, ate the turkey by candlelight and eventually went to bed by candlelight.

Happy Christmas to the three pioneering women !

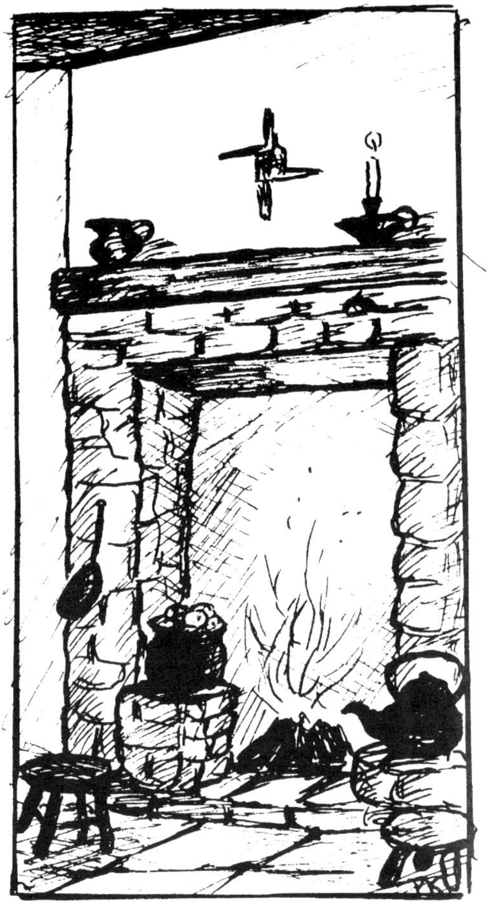

AFTER CHRISTMAS

Our first visitor on St. Stephen's Day was the Electricity Company's Engineer and relating our Christmas Day plight, he checked our new installations declaring the fault to be on the main supply pole outside, which he climbed, did magic things with pliers and screwdriver and our electricity supply was restored.

Appreciating his visit during the Christmas holiday period, we parted the best of friends wishing each other the compliments of the Season.

In neighbouring houses a large candle was lit on Christmas Eve and placed in the window, glowing each night until New Year's eve when it was replaced by another to welcome in the New Year. The sequence was that this too glowed brightly until Little Christmas Eve (which we knew as Twelfth Night) the sign for the end of this sacred and joyful period : decorations were taken down and packed away for another year.

St. Stephen's Day brought us another new experience - the Wren Boys. It was an old tradition still retained, although brought up to date to fit the present day ! The origin was that local children would dress up in a strange assortment of old clothes of odd sizes, black their faces, or wear full masks made from material with holes cut out for eyes and mouth and went visiting in the district, chanting the rhyme

> The wran, the wran, the king of all birds,
> St. Stephen's Day was caught in the furze;
> Up with the kettle and down with the pan
> And give us some money to bury the wran.

The girls and boys who called on us were more commercially minded. One child rolled up in a car to make his house-to-house collection saying his mother would pick him up in ten minutes, could he go first to do his piece Not recognising him we said, 'Come in. You're welcome. Where do you live?' He named a village nine miles away and said his mother had brought him because it was raining and he had lots of cousins here. Unabashed he continued, 'This is a great townland for the Wren Boys'. He certainly was not a shy child - others we had found could be shy in our presence.

Fair play to the children who did step down into our kitchen giving spirited, if sometimes tuneless, renderings of modern pop songs, familiar Irish airs, and, with a clattering of feet, they danced sometimes unaccompanied but occasionally to the sound of a penny whistle played with various degrees of competence.

When they had gone we reminisced. 'I remember once going out at Halloween as Red Riding Hood. My red dressing gown was tied up to make a hood and the rest as the cloak. We thought we were great. We even had a halfpenny tramcar ride to collect further along the road, where generous aunties dispensed apples, oranges and sometimes sweets.'

Heather added, 'Yes, I remember Halloween "dressing up" in my Aunt's clothes - she was in amateur dramatics, you know - a well worn brown fox fur which trailed to the ground after being wrapped round my neck twice till I could hardly see over it. The hat was made of glorious purple velvet, its size came over my ears and nearly met the fox fur coming up. The coat, or in this case, a jacket fitted where it touched and the whole outfit was topped with a large handbag, big enough to hold the apples, oranges and sweets 'gifted' by the friends who had to suffer 'the party piece'. What a vision!

Between Christmas and New Year we spent time enjoying the relative peace of the house and exploration of the many little roads which almost always led down to the sea.

We noticed that at night it was never totally dark. A torch was carried so that we could be seen on the road - there were no pavements.

On clear moonlight nights looking over the fields to the sea it was silver and fishing boats were visible by their navigation lights. Because of the distance they appeared close together and resembled another small village with Christmas Lights showing under a sky ablaze with a myriad of stars.

This Christmas was 'different' from our usual ones and New Year's Eve was even more so. To Scots, New Year's Eve or Hogmanay as we call it, is a time of mixed emotions; memories, sad and happy, of loved ones no longer with us or far afield in other lands and it's also a time to look forward. There is of course the customary revelry at midnight 'first footin' friends. But this year for we three with a glass in hand it was a case of thinking of our friends, wishing them a Guid New Year and toasting ourselves health and happiness ahead in our new chosen life.

Early in January the work recommenced. Painting had to be done on walls and the new window frames. Around the house concrete paths and patio areas were laid, interspersed with circular and square flower beds.

The two of us took part in all of this activity painting the outside of the house and even going up on the roof to do the chimneys. Showers of rain didn't dampen our enthusiasm but we did find the paint slid down the surface. Drat it, the job had to be done again. So much for manufacturers' claims of 'superior products' - shades of 'new', 'super', 'ultra' descriptions as in the soap powder ads.

This then was our baptism of fire in house painting - you have heard of the phrase getting on like .....

Frank, a friend from Dublin, came to make fitted wardrobes, shelving and vanity units in bedrooms. He quietly beavered away whilst noisy hectic activity took place around him.

By March it was time to take delivery of new carpets and we marvelled at the skill and speed of the carpet layer - yes, singular, one man did a marvellous job.

Then it was a case of curtains hung, beds in place, hospitality trays in the bedrooms ready for guests, public rooms furnished, pictures hung, vases in place, and generally all was well. We surveyed with pleasure our new home inside and out and felt justified in what we had decided all those months ago and which we had now achieved.

Since arriving in November, postman Festy King had a busy time delivering cards for 'Your New Home', Chris-Ann's ninety-first birthday, Christmas and New Year, Heather's birthday in February and then St. Patrick's Day in March.

Delivery of mail took the form of Festy in his van pulling up on the gravel, sounding horn, and we'd go out to collect, passing the time of day and commenting on the weather in local description of 'A soft class of a day', or maybe 'Sure it's a pet day'.

For people living in rural parts of any country the arrival of the postman heralds a highlight of their day. He brings news, good, bad, sometimes indifferent but as he knows his recipients he gives comment on the outside world. Messages from other neighbours can be passed on, 'How is Paddy Michael in hospital?' : 'What did you think of the pony show?' : 'My, it was a powerful market day over and beyond'.

A real sort of social worker is the postman. We are sure the change of name of our cottage featured largely in such conversations.

The Red Cottage which had been popular and successful was now under new management. We had pondered over a new name, wanting to make our own mark. The decision was Brandyburn Cottage, the first half of the word coming from, as we have said earlier, the Irish Gazetteer's description of the road between Clifden and Roundstone where it was described as the Brandy and Soda road because of the exhilarating air ! In Scotland a wee burn is often a tributary and so was the road from Ballyconneely to our house. The two words were put together and Brandyburn Cottage came to life.

Now that we had a habitable house ready for visitors, two friends from Glasgow came over, via Liverpool and then driving the 200 miles from Dublin to Connemara. This was a first visit for Lena and Marsali to Connemara and they were greatly impressed by all the breath-taking vistas. They spent happy hours exploring in Marsali's car, coming back to Brandyburn to try out our 'home cooking' in the evening, congratulating us on all our achievements.

IT ALWAYS RAINS IN THE WEST - NOT S0

How often we were told that in Dublin ! Yes, there were some wild days but so many more 'pet days' made up for them. How many times do 'townies' eat out of doors in the Winter ? Our patios were sheltered from any breeze, bar a westerly wind, and mince and tatties taste great eaten out of doors.

The sun rose behind Errisbeg, the mountain looking down on Roundstone, some nine miles distant. As the back of Brandyburn Cottage faced due south, the sunshine moved along the whole length of the house and to two Scots this free lighting and solar central heating was very acceptable ! Early in the morning before the sun came into view, the rays caught transatlantic flights heading for Shannon Airport. The vapour trails were deep pink, the plane itself resembling a rosy cigar. From their lofty transport, what did the sleepy-eyed passengers think of this bird's eye view of Ireland? To some it would be a first visit, perhaps to the land of their forefathers, and to others it would be an emigrant's home-coming. Surely nature's patchwork must have added to the excitement and anticipation of their visit.

Looking towards the village, the Twelve Pins made a wonderful backdrop. Some days they were blue and hazy but on others they could be dark and forbidding. In his distinctive landscapes the artist Paul Henry captured such changing moods. Some unkind visitors quoted the saying that if you could see the hills clearly it was going to rain and if you couldn't see them, it was raining !

Skirting the foothills of the Twelve Pins is the main road between Galway and Clifden carrying the heavy goods vehicles, buses and, in the summer season, many cars from many countries. It is only fair to say that the foreign cars can be seen frequently in the out-of-season months. This main link has been widened and straightened out since Heather first went to Galway but there is still the surprise of a pot-hole. Houses are well scattered across the countryside and close to them ridged land can be seen which shows where the owner had 'lazy beds' for growing potatoes. The principle of 'lazy beds' is akin to a sandwich - seaweed for fertiliser is spread on a straight width of the ground and the seed potatoes placed on top. Then the sods are cut along both edges of the seaweed bed and, grass-side down, they are set on top of the potatoes. The shallow trench on either side is made deeper by removing the soil and placing it on top of the upside down sods, the trench becoming a drainage system. Arable land is scarce as it is so stony and only very small areas can be cultivated by a family, if at all possible.

Our exploration of the neighbourhood we put down to research for the benefit of our future guests. This took us to north of Clifden which showed a different terrain from that around Ballyconneely. Now we could see some trees. There were no trees down our road. No, no - we tell a lie. We inherited one in our garden, a fir tree, which surprisingly grew very well. The ground was shallow and the Atlantic gales hit hard. Eventually we noticed our tree had developed a distinct list to port and action had to be taken at once. Again this was an item for the Gerry list and an immediate rescue took place. He got hold of a piece of blue rope from somewhere and wound it twice round the tree about three feet from the top, securing the two ends around a convenient boulder embedded in the long grass. The problem was solved and the tree continued to look good and grow.

Two winters later in January, Heather found a Christmas tree being blown around the garden, thought it strange and mentioned it to Amy. Looking out the window we saw we were now the doubtful proud owners of the only topless tree in the neighbourhood. The rope had acted as a saw every time the tree was shaken in a strong wind and finally the top flew off. Some establishments have topless waitresses and we were originally different!

Another rescue operation by Gerry was when the original inherited wooden clothes pole finally collapsed. As an essential piece of equipment for drying the washing, a strong replacement was necessary, so Gerry got to work with bits of wood of assorted sizes. When finished it had the unfortunate appearance of a gallows. It was beside the land-drainage trench which at one time was overgrown with grasses and later on caused the downfall of our friend Marie from the States. She was helping us to chase marauding cows, didn't see the ditch and fell in. After we got the new clothes pole it was forever after called 'The Hanging Gallows at Marie's Creek'.

North of Clifden we discovered the National Park. It was actually opened in 1980 for the benefit of visitors and the local people. We always enjoyed, as did our guests, visits to Connemara National Park with the Diamond Mountain presiding over the landscape. The Visitor

Centre mounted displays explaining the archaeology and geology of the area, the fauna and flora, along with excellent photographs taken by the Board of Works in illustration.

The approach to the Park by car is on a feat of road engineering, travelling upwards on a broad swathe carved out of the hillside with a few near-hairpin bends. And what vistas as we travel to the top - they change at each corner. After parking the car we walk down a short way to sample all the Centre has to offer the visitor. Those on foot walk up a short entrance-way from the village of Letterfrack.

Two well-marked nature walks lead off from the Centre, Ellis Wood downwards beside the waterfall and stream, picturesque in springtime with a carpet of wild flowers, and Sraffanaboy trail leading upwards on to the Diamond itself passing contented grazing Connemara ponies. Adjacent to the Centre, a video theatre tells of the Park's history and achievements.

In the Centre there is a small kitchen where visitors can avail of the facilities of electric kettle and a ring for heating a saucepan. Probably many a baby's bottle has been warmed up on the ring. An indoor picnic area is available, furnished with traditional Irish sugan chairs and beautiful polished tables hewn from trees. Ample outdoor picnic tables are also provided.

At the village of Letterfrack stands a large building which in its early life had been a Reformatory run by the Christian Brothers for young offenders. Some of the boys came from cities such as Dublin and to young lads from a city, the country itself was punishment enough. Never having seen a cow before, the sight of one struck terror in many of them. Seemingly in the early 1900s an epidemic swept through the area and it is tragic to see the names listed on a solitary cross of so many of the boys and the Brothers who had died that winter. A large communal grave in a secluded clearing marks their sad deaths.

Happily this building is now used by Connemara West as a Community Centre, housing doctors' surgery, a training centre which is affiliated to Galway Regional Technical College for wood-turning and the manufacture of furniture, an adjoining area displaying the extent of their craftsmanship. The local radio station, Connemara Community Radio, transmits from the Centre, the work of the operators being voluntary. Many of the local people have had the personal thrill of a birthday greeting or message of congratulations and choice of music sent to them over the air waves. This is another line of communication of local news and forthcoming events in the district. In such a rural area, ready availability of tools, seeds, fertilisers, fencing and building materials are on hand at the well-run Co-operative venture, an adjunct of the Centre.

A popular beach quite close to Brandyburn is down by the safe harbour of Bunowen. Overlooking the bay and harbour is a ruined castle originally owned by the Clan O'Flaherty which Clan ruled Connemara. As a very young girl, Grace O'Malley, the Pirate Queen of Connemara, was married to a descendant of the O'Flahertys, she herself was the chieftain's daughter of the seafaring Clan O'Malley.

Grace O'Malley, or Graunaile in Irish, was a true pirate queen; she traded with Spain, raided English shipping and, it seems, any other country's shipping misguided enough to enter Irish waters. She spent time in various other O'Flaherty castles and, when necessary, fought hard in their defence. In later life she went to London to make her peace with Queen Elizabeth I to secure the inheritance of her sons when Connaught was conquered by the English. Women's Rights never gave her a thought!

On the Clifden side of Ballyconneely was our own favourite beach, the Coral Strand: not sandy and not the usual shell type but comprised of the remains of calcified seaweed. It's well worth spending time beach-combing. Much of our happy stolen time from land-ladying was spent in the warm, clear water. Due to atmospheric conditions, distinct pink-toned currents could occasionally be seen. If an artist depicted this in a picture it would possibly be considered artistic licence.

The Coral Strand has a popular lay-by and coaches are frequently pulling in to allow their passengers pour down on to the beach to search for unusual shells and small pieces of 'coral'. One day we watched as a coach stopped and its passengers, all Spanish teenagers, tumbled out. They had seen this wonderful white beach, the calm azure sea, the tiny waves curling over on to the shore, all under a cloudless sky. They were running down the beach pulling off clothes to reveal Mediterranean tanned bodies in stunning colourful beachwear. After sitting for some time in an overwarm coach, the tempting sea would seem to be the answer to their prayers. It was only when they ran into the cool sea that the illusion was shattered - the temperature of the sea was not like the Mediterranean as their shrieks confirmed!

Basking there in the sun we invariably thought of our friends back in Dublin who had said 'It always rains in the West'. In long spells of dry weather combined with the increase in house building, water shortages did occur and requests were issued to conserve water. If the building upturn were to continue, plans would have to be put in hand for increased water capacity. It always rains in the West, indeed!

Perhaps this gives an all-perfect picture of our life in the West. Of course there were bad spells, rain and wind, and when it was a gale it was the full force from the Atlantic. We realised how much salt was carried in the wind as at times it could leave a thin layer on the windows and even the flowers in the garden would be burnt brown. This aerial hazard is also bad news for cars which mostly are not in garages. Amy's car which had clocked up an enormous mileage and sustained scratches on the cellulose from stone chippings, etc. was very badly attacked by the salt-laden wind, so much so that the rusting developed into holes. There were so many perforations we christened the car Teabag.

There were quite a few 'clapped out bangers' which eventually gave up and were frequently just left to rot away. In time we witnessed the ignominy of Teabag being towed by tractor across a rocky field to the back of its new owner's house. There was no road to its destination, petering out about 50 yards short, but Teabag was to rest there as a 'shed' for storing bales of hay.

Snow and frost doesn't happen too often but when it does the countryside looks lovely. Once when it had been very hard frost, an inlet of the sea looked wonderful at very low tide with brown seaweed covered rocks topped with thick sparkling ice. It gave the impression of a giant baker's shop window displaying iced cakes.

The winter we had snow on the ground for two days, Gerry's little Jack Russell called Lady got a surprise when she came running to meet us, she couldn't stop and we had to jump out of the way to let her skid by. She tried it again and as she slid past a second time we swore we heard her say 'Wheeeeee!'.

It is a hard life in the winter when the weather is bad. Most cottages and houses use solid fuel and the turf stacks are out in the open weighted down with ropes and fishing nets. It can be a battle against the elements to fill a box of turf and bring it indoors to dry.

In winter with very little grazing on the poor stone-filled land, the cattle and horses had to be fed hay. The farmers saved what little they could grow themselves, as to buy in supplies was costly, but it had to be done when their own stocks were finished. It was common to see a haystack on top of a pair of legs as the farmer walked along the road, bending into the wind, carrying the heavy load roped on to his back. If he was lucky enough to have a car, the hay could be put in the open boot and the cattle followed as a donkey with a carrot.

For days on end the sea can be too rough for fishing. The only compensation is the beauty of its wildness along a rocky coastline, but that brings no joy to the fisherman who has to earn a living from the sea.

Perhaps being 'blow-ins' we tended to look towards the beauty and majesty of the mountains, land and sea whereas the locals who were born in Connemara have had a tough upbringing, walking to the village, to school, to church because there was no car and no public transport. Perhaps they are a more tolerant and contented people.

READY FOR BUSINESS

To test our abilities and at the same time say 'Thank you' to friends who had given us moral support and encouragement we decided to open officially at Easter by inviting ten of them from Dublin. A two-edged invitation. They would be guinea pigs for the weekend and in turn would give us honest criticism of a weekend at Brandyburn.

It was a heatwave ! Yes, despite all the gloomy remarks of people that it always rained in Connemara, the sun shone continuously and showed the area at its brightest and best. Nowhere is there air and atmosphere so clear, skies so expressive and sea so blue as in Connemara on its best behaviour.

First to arrive were Pierce and Eileen. When Heather and her mother settled in Dublin in 1954 they were fortunate to have Pierce and Eileen for neighbours who extended a warm welcome and an enduring friendship which exists to the present day. Over the years they were indoctrinated into some of the Scottish happenings such as Hogmanay where the traditional customs were first of all explained to new friends and neighbours who joined Heather and Chris-Ann to welcome in the New Year. Many such happy evenings followed.

Audrey and Bobby came and as we welcomed them Audrey couldn't contain herself - 'Show us everything. We've been patiently awaiting this day since you left Dublin in November'. Bobby, in his own quiet way admired what was our new home and paid particular appreciation to Frank's joinery work.

Frank and Joy joined in the oh's and ah's. Joy who had been a bit apprehensive of Frank undertaking his part in the renovations, a retired man with asthma, forgave him his nights away from home but knew he had been well cared for at Brandyburn. She was always thankful when she met Frank at Heuston Station in Dublin after his weekly visits to the west and to realise he was none the worse of the physical efforts of joinery and travel.

Margaret and Scott were visiting us from Paisley, Scotland. Margaret and Amy were friends and Margaret for many years had come to consider first Dublin then Connemara a home from home. In this her first visit to Brandyburn she brought her grandson Scott aged 9 years, a city child who had never spent a holiday in the country. He was in his element at all the new experiences and didn't heed grandma's chidings about safety in the fields and cleanliness as he romped about in the boggy ground.

For a more professional appraisal of our weekend hosting of the party Tommy and Ita brought their expertise as established caterers. While they catered for many in Dublin society, our efforts were very low key by comparison. Nevertheless both were generous in their comments. 'A word in your ear,' said Tommy. 'You don't serve enough potatoes. The meals were excellent apart from that.'

Our friends were enchanted as they followed our suggestions for sight-seeing and they returned for the evening dinner full of the joys of life. Starting with afternoon tea on the Friday of their arrival, through dinner, bed and breakfast until late Monday afternoon, we had a very happy congenial party. After dinner we joined in the coffee and chat in the sitting room and this was our modus operanda for all the evenings at Brandyburn, hearing of our guests' activities and outings and we contributing with yarns and stories.

None of our friends had seen Brandyburn Cottage before but knew from contact over the past months that we had been renovating the house to our requirements. They plied us with questions and we explained that basically the overall shape of the house was the same as it had been except for an additional porch built on at the west to protect from prevailing winds. The red roof of the cottage had gone, having been replaced with black slates. New doors and windows were of teak set into the white painted walls.

Bulk-head lighting had been installed at the corners of the building and over the kitchen's half door, casting a welcoming pool of light across the road and aiding 'homegoers' from the village 'after hours'.

That Easter, with its heatwave, saw Bobby excuse himself from wife, Audrey and friends Frank and Joy as they walked the beach at Gurteen Bay. Dodging behind a rock he divested himself of his clothes and streaked into the sea 'in the nip'. On later visits he always had his swimming togs with him and never failed to enjoy his swims in the Atlantic.

So only one real complaint from the weekend - 'You didn't serve enough potatoes'. We held our heads low for this was a serious complaint in Ireland, famous for its consumption of potatoes.

Thank you again to Audrey and Bobby, Tommy and Ita, Pierce and Eileen, Margaret and Scott, Frank and Joy. Never again on their subsequent visits did they go short of potatoes in Brandyburn.

THE FIRST PAYING GUESTS

Following the departure on Easter Monday of our guinea pig friends, we were ready for action and two days later on a rather miserable misty day, a mini-bus pulled up to the door. Excitement in Brandyburn Cottage – could this be our first paying guests ? It was a family from America, Mum, Dad, Gran, two college boys and a younger school boy. They had landed at Shannon Airport and rented a mini-bus for their tour of Western Ireland.

After leaving luggage in their rooms they came to the sitting room to enjoy a turf fire and a welcome cup of tea. The two older boys decided to walk up the little hill across the road to see 'the castle' at the top. This in actual fact was the water tower for our water supply, but as it was shrouded in mist it looked mysteriously intriguing. Usually the view from the top produced a spectacular panorama. In the rolling mist the boys later returned to the Cottage exhilarated but very damp, leaving their trainers in the porch to dry out from their walk across the boggy land. Sitting round the fire drinking hot chocolate they recounted their 'climb to the castle', and saying how the cottage, turf fires, rolling mist and the castle were 'neat' and 'real Ireland'.

The youngest boy, Carlton aged about 12, took great delight in coming to the kitchen door to ask questions. We suspected the pretty tile on the door proclaiming 'Keep out Mum's cooking' was an invitation to him. His first question arose after seeing the hospitality tray in his room. 'How many cups of tea do you get from one tea bag?' We said we had never tried to find out and off he went. Twenty minutes later he was back all smiles to tell us he could get six cups ! Once again there was the by now familiar knock at the door and this time he was clutching the hot water bottle from his bedroom - a great discovery as he had never seen one before. We explained it was to keep him warm in bed but this time the hot water went into the bottle and was not for drinking !

Time for dinner and the family settled in the dining room. They all enjoyed their first meal in Ireland, Carlton instructing us in a low voice out of the side of his mouth to 'go easy on the greens' as we served the vegetables. This drew a look of exasperation from his mother as over a long period of time she had been encouraging him to eat more green vegetables, but it was all good natured fun, the family teasing Carlton and his eyes rolling to us looking for mock sympathy !

Serving coffee in the sitting room and talking with them about Ireland and America, we discovered that the League family came from Maryland. The evening passed very pleasantly for all of us and as jet lag was beginning to catch up they weren't too late in going to bed. Carlton was too tired even to fill his new toy, the hot water bottle. The following morning after a hearty and healthy breakfast we waved goodbye to them as friends setting off on their tour of Ireland.

Heather has had a 'pen pal', Alice, in Maryland since school days and when writing to her, she mentioned that our first paying guests had been American and came from Maryland. From Alice came a quick question 'Where in Maryland?' Again another letter from us telling where.

Heather feels she is not accident prone but incident prone. Still she was not prepared for the news that Alice had a friend in the small township from which the Brandyburn guests had come. When Alice 'phoned her friend she asked if she happened to know the League family.

Not only did her friend know them as nearby neighbours but said, 'Oh yes, they are on holiday in Ireland and I remember you told me your friend, Heather, had a Guest House, but as I didn't know the address I couldn't tell the Leagues where.' She was amazed to learn that they had chanced on that same Guest House on their first day in Ireland.

An extraordinary coincidence which was to bring a sequel some time later.

THE GARDEN - NOT OF EDEN BECAUSE NO APPLE TREES : NO TREES

As soon as possible after our arrival in Ballyconneely we emptied the trailer and started planting which proved to be no easy task. As mostly the soil was very shallow, as indeed it is throughout Connemara, our ground had barely been cultivated, so a small flower bed was dug to 'heel in' the plants in the hope that through time a garden would materialise. It was with fury that Heather discovered cows and calves, having come over the boundary wall, were tramping through the 'garden', and always having had a great fear of cows it was left to Amy who went out to take action waving a stick and gently saying 'Come along boys'. 'Boys?' thought Heather, 'Something wrong there'.

Boys or no boys Amy got them over the wall. Two hours later they had returned with more damage done to the mini garden and so the chase was on again. Still furious at the damage being done and conquering her fear, muttering to herself, Heather chased the last two beasts back over the wall, the little calf going over head first. Feeling guilty at her cruelty to animals, she spent the rest of the day wondering how much it would cost to pay the farmer if the calf had broken its neck!

During our first year at Brandyburn most of our time was taken up settling into Guest House activities but, as we were keen to have some colourful flowers, we had kept the old bath, three hand basins and two loos which had been replaced during the renovations. Along with an old fashioned porcelain sink brought from Dublin, they were placed out in this new back 'garden of the future'. These objects were filled with fine turf, what bits of soil we could dig up and bedding plants put in. We reckoned London had its Kew Gardens - we had our Loo Gardens.

At the front of the house an existing narrow low trough was raised to two feet high and filled with soil and turf. Augmented by tea leaves and coffee grounds, eventually it produced good shows of bedding flowers.

'Out of Season' we became proficient scavengers, on the beach and land. Our target was old, disused builders' barrows. If the bottoms had rotted away we found pieces of caravan roofs which had been smashed in a storm. Taking home the spoils, Amy jumped on them to flatten and shape and, hey presto, new bottoms in the barrow, fill it up and it was ready to plant flowers. In our beach-scavenging we found vertebrae of sharks and a whale. The latter made stools to sit on in the garden, and the smaller shark vertebrae became candle sticks and attractive lamps, all these interesting items making good talking points.

On scavenging hunts, our little friend, Lady, the Jack Russell terrier, joined us but was more interested in rabbit holes than getting her feet and under-carriage wet. We had to pull her out of many holes by the back end, she strenuously protesting at our interrupting her activity. It didn't stop her - she just went looking for another rabbit hole.

Travelling to Galway one day Heather spotted the shafts of a barrow sticking up out of a ditch beside a wood. Always ready to add to the beauty of the garden she stopped the car, scrambled down the ditch but found the old discarded barrow to be too heavy to get it on to the road. Arriving home she told Amy of it so a couple of days later the two of them took off in Heather's Fiesta. Yes, the barrow was still there - and they manhandled it up to the car, but it wouldn't fit in. Back it went down into the ditch. Not giving in easily, a week later they were once again on the way to Galway, stopping the car at the barrow spot and, yes, it was just waiting for them. Deciding to collect it on the way home from Galway after a big grocery shopping, the barrow would go in the boot of Amy's larger car and the problem would be solved. We picked up a young man at Oughterard. Oh, perhaps that could be better rephrased ! As there is no railway, and buses run infrequently from Galway to Clifden, quite often there are hitch hikers on the road; not back-packers, but locals who hope someone with a car will come along. This day a young man, a 'townie' by his appearance, thumbed a lift at Oughterard and we stopped. He climbed into the car and off we set, he telling us his life story. He was a medical student heading for Clifden and then a little further north to join friends who had a house there and would spend the weekend with them. So it was that the miles passed quickly in his company and, as we approached our barrow goal, we told him we wanted to stop for a couple of minutes to collect a barrow which we intended to recycle. He seemed a bit puzzled as there was neither shop nor house in view, but said he would get out and give us a hand. We had first of all to transfer the contents of the boot into the back of the car before retrieving our prospective plant holder. The young man ferried the parcels and we stowed them away leaving enough room to fit him in too. When the point was reached to go down into the ditch to get the barrow our passenger didn't seem to be fittingly attired in camel coat, yellow gloves and suede shoes ! As the saying goes, 'fair play to him', he got into the act and the three of us puffed, groaned and strained to get the barrow up from the ditch and into the boot of the car. Covering the last three miles to Clifden, our young man was strangely silent and after expressing his gratitude for the lift hastily left us. We always suspected he would dine out for some time on the story of the two grey haired ladies who had him haul an old wheel-less, bottom-less, rusty old barrow out of a ditch and put it in the boot of their car to take home. And they seemed such a nice intelligent pair!

The next winter and spring we progressed from barrows. We had initially made a rockery from the path at the back of the house down to the level of the rest of the ground, a relatively flat area of rough field grass. Having earmarked this area for our vegetable garden (oh, yes, we had high hopes of being self sufficient) we had a consultation with Gerry. What was required was cover the area with sand, then a layer of seaweed followed by loose turf from the bog. All this would eventually bed down and produce reasonably good tilth for our vegetables.

The load of sand was brought in and raked over. Then came the seaweed left in piles to be spread over the sand.

That night, four South African friends of Amy were staying before travelling to Cork. As they hadn't seen Amy for some years, there was plenty to talk about before going to bed after midnight. When we were closing down the house a guest, who was a close friend, came to us in a distressed state saying she had been reading in bed and that there were 'things', 'bugs', 'animals', jumping about in her room, were all over the walls and were coming in the window. Well now - she didn't drink, so what was she on about ? We went to her room, closed the window and yes there truly were 'things', 'bugs', 'animals', jumping about all over the place. We immediately transferred her into our only vacant room and calmed her down, ready for sleep. We raced outside to see if we could learn where they were coming from and to our horror saw the wall was black with the 'things'. They were about an inch long, black and the inside had the appearance of a small shrimp. By the light of the moon we could see them all around. We presumed it must have been something similar to the swarm of ladybirds which had covered an area in England some years before but, as nothing could be achieved until daylight, we too went off to bed.

Sneaking into the offending bedroom early in the morning we discovered the 'things' were less active and indeed most appeared dead. Once more an item for the Gerry list so a couple were scooped up as evidence and put in a match box.

Normal Guest House service was maintained. Our friend appeared for breakfast bright-eyed and bushy-tailed none the worse of her previous night's alarming experience. Gerry came in to see what our problem was and so we displayed the dead 'things' in the box and told him the tale. As we told him about this swarm in the bedroom and the wall outside, we saw 'that certain smile' come around his mouth and we knew our problem was, to Gerry and probably the rest of the community, a natural phenomenon.

The 'things' were sand hoppers and had come out of our little mountains of seaweed. Being attracted to light they came towards the open window and leapt in, but without the support of their natural environment they just died. After a couple of days when the seaweed was spread, there were no more live 'things'. Talking with our neighbour we found the sand hoppers had also invaded her territory, being attracted by the glow from the television set. She had to seal up her kitchen door and stick a note on it to tell the family to come in by the front door. What, we wondered, could the 'things' have wanted to see - a David Attenborough nature programme or maybe gardening?

Each year we expanded our garden. The main section, now cultivated, produced good organic vegetables and to our excitement, the first cabbage we lifted weighed eleven pounds. Potatoes, carrots, white turnips, peas, beetroot, two kinds of lettuce, courgettes, cabbage and cauliflowers all proved successful. We had to abandon the latter two as nasty green caterpillars always beat us to the eating. Our radishes grew so well that we couldn't cope with our crop and left them to flower. That was a bonus as we used them in floral decorations ! Parsley was another very successful crop and the best mint we ever had came from Inishbofin Island with a friend who had been there on holiday. We have heard of transplanting, but .....

Herbaceous borders materialised and gave us a riot of colour. This success was due in no small measure to the thoughtfulness and generosity of our friends who came to visit, plus the fact that the Gulf Stream passed up this coast and as palm trees were in evidence, the climate couldn't have been all bad. There were always plants in the boot of cars along with luggage which enabled us to have a 'friendship' garden.

Gardens in Connemara were not top priority in the way of life, essential vegetables were. We reckon our efforts encouraged others gradually to put more colour into their lives.

The garden was hard manual work and there were occasions when we ran out of time and had to get help from a neighbour. Sean King and sometimes his son John came to our rescue. They were human machines at the digging ! Cutting turf on the bog must build up muscles.

To maintain our home-made garden soil, Heather hitched up the trailer to her Fiesta (known as Rosie) and went off to a mushroom farm to collect spent compost. The day after it was spread, giant mushrooms appeared!

Then a friend introduced us to the owners of a pony trekking and riding school so that we could ease their over-load of excess horse manure. Once again a trailer job. On arrival we were astounded to see the most beautiful proud peacocks strutting around. Something we didn't expect to encounter in the wilds of Connemara.

As the years went by, we drew seaweed regularly to enrich the soil. There was no doubt that it gave the best results. As we could reasonably collect it ourselves we made many trips down to a little bay which was accessible by car and trailer. Lady liked this exercise too and as we did our navvying, she ran through the long grass in the adjoining old cemetery. In this peaceful part of County Galway the fast pace of modern life seemed very far away. It's no wonder that visitors come to relax in unspoilt natural surroundings. Yet, even that peaceful little cemetery was touched by the sadness of War, as it was the last resting place of a few airmen and sailors. The sea had given them up to this haven.

We were intent, perhaps even obsessed, on making a garden yet all around is Mother Nature's garden. We marvelled at the profusion of wild flowers, primrose, yellow flag iris, cowslips, stonecrops, celandines, pimpernels, wood avens, herb robert, loosestrife, violets, et al. We determined we'd have our own wild flower garden.

Our land was, therefore, divided up giving rock garden, stepping down into the vegetable patch, edged by a drainage ditch - Marie's Creek -and through some rough privet and escallonia bushes to an undulating grass covered area which had to be partially tamed, leaving space for the wild flowers to grow undisturbed.

The grass taming gave us some fun. Buying a scythe we tried to wield it but as Heather said after a couple of abortive attempts which might have resulted in cutting off our legs beneath the knees, 'Let's ask Joe for a lesson'. Joe came and watching us with a painful expression on his face he was much relieved when we admitted defeat, begging him to use his expertise. In no time at all he had scythed the ground we suggested.

Joe is a busy man, a man of many country talents from breeding cattle and Connemara ponies to building and we couldn't add to his work-load by asking him to scythe our grass on a regular basis, so we bought a Black and Dekker Rotary mower. This was extremely successful - we just put it in the long grass and let it fight its way out ! This method did not impress the Black & Dekker salesman when next we were speaking, but for us, it was effective. The cut long grass was recycled to passing cattle or those in a nearby field so no waste.

The vista down the garden looked good but it still needed definition at points. There were a few rocky outcrops beside our topless tree which called for pockets of plants.

Our friend, Brendan, gave us bluebell bulbs. A donation of New Zealand flax from Kay McEverley of Cashel House was planted at the boundary wall : some primroses and wild garlic went in to the damp area close to the drainage ditch which dried out in summer.

There were already wild pyramidal orchids, full flowering buttercups and bright ox-eye daisies in the ground. The orchids are very precious and gave us a great thrill to see them in the garden. Washing, perfumed by meadow-sweet and drying above wild orchids, seems like indecent luxury.

Needing so many more varieties, we used one St. Patrick's Day to seek out more plant life for our wild garden. We needed some gunera (a plant looking like very wild, large leaf rhubarb) to be planted in selected spots along the boundary wall : some dainty flowered cowslips, lacy ferns: the tall elegant orange coloured montbretia : and some rhododendrons.

Our foray into collecting rhodos, gunera, fuchsias, etc. went very well and we headed for home. It had been a very cold day and we were dressed like the Michelin man, woolly tea-cosy-like hats on the heads and green wellies on the feet with a definite layered look under anoraks. Amy spied a nice large clump of montbretia by the roadside so we stopped. Heather walked along a bit to get a handsome fern and left Amy to it. Amy shouted she was having difficulty getting the spade to go into the compacted ground so tackled the job with a fork. There was a loud yell and when Heather looked up, there stood Amy dripping wet, unable to see through her specs, mud and grass all over her hat and a water spout arching to the other side of the narrow road. She had punctured a shallow-buried plastic water pipe ! After initial shock and hysterical laughter we made a hasty retreat. We long laughed at the picture of Amy and the day her spirit was dampened.

Still nursing a guilty conscience about the water pipe, one day we were surprised to see Sergeant Kelly with slow measured step coming down our garden path. He approached us with his usual serious countenance. We were busy repotting plants on a table out of doors. We glanced at each other. At our feet beneath the table were two buckets of stone chippings which we had purloined from the quarry along the road. Of course these chippings were the property of the County Council and not meant to be used by gardeners. Were we about to be apprehended, caught red-handed, disgraced? We could see the headlines in the Connacht Tribune.

Attack is the best form of defence. 'Hello there Sergeant Kelly', we chorused, hoping he wouldn't notice our booty. 'We're propagating our geraniums. Aren't they good cuttings ? This hormone rooting powder is great stuff. Do you use it?'

Knowing he was a keen gardener we chattered on, asking advice on this and that putting off the time when we would hear the purpose of his visit.

'Good news, wasn't it?' he beamed. 'What did you think when you heard it?'

We were still mystified and blurted out, 'Oh yes - wasn't it a surprise?' hoping to cover our ignorance.

"Here it is then. The cheque for five hundred pounds. Thanks for supporting the golf club draw. It's nice when someone local wins'. So saying he handed over the envelope. 'Well, must get back on duty'.

With a quick glance at our efforts in propagating plants, he went on his way leaving us speechless. Recovering we called after him, 'Thanks - thank you Sergeant Kelly'.

Relieved that we were not having to GO DIRECTLY TO JAIL, we downed tools and returning to the house for the sherry bottle and glasses repaired to the patio to celebrate our good fortune.

HANDS ACROSS THE SEA

A friendship which started back in our Dublin days was with Dorothy and Marie from Florida who had contacted us through the International Federation of Business & Professional Women's Clubs of which we were members. We had discovered many interests in common and so it was inevitable we should meet again this time at Brandyburn. Also staying with us was Margaret from Paisley, Jean from Dublin and Florence and Frank from Bristol.

In Florida, Dorothy and Marie are prodigious in their output of handcrafts, raising many thousands of dollars for their respective churches, Methodist and Roman Catholic. So after dinner. we would all be given materials and with Dorothy directing operations we talked, we stitched, we listened to Frank accompanying us on the piano and completed tapestry squares of Christmas motifs, making up hanging decorations with the letters JOY and NOEL, and finished off with tassels and bells. The time came when Frank was so curious about what we were doing that he forsook the piano and getting his pattern, wools and needle he soon had an output to match the ladies. At Christmas in each of our houses we bring out these decorations and recall the pleasant time when the eight of us were beavering away.

To Dorothy and Marie on their Autumn visit, the hedgerows provided amusement as up and down the boreens they went with plastic boxes picking blackberries - in Scotland we call them brambles.

Marie would come back chortling, 'I fell into the ditch again and nearly lost them all. It was just like the time I fell into Marie's Creek,' she hollered. 'Drat them cows.'

They couldn't get over the profusion of berries and all for free.

'Gee, in our stores they would charge many dollars a kilo', added Dorothy.

The kitchen became a hive of industry as the four of us prepared the brambles, weighed out apples and sugar, sculpted pies with pastry, Irish and American recipes, more brambles were pureed and frozen for a later ice cream making session. Blackberry ice cream was a 'hot' favourite with our guests.

Amy encouraged Heather to tell her story of making crab apple jelly in Dublin and no matter how often the story was told it always ended in helpless laughter.

'Well, you see,' related Heather, 'back in Dublin I had been given this large bag of crab apples and wanted to use them to make jelly. The only problem was I didn't have a jelly bag to strain the pulp so I went down to the local shops but no luck. None to be had. Then a stroke of pure genius hit me. Improvise I thought and sailed into our local Ladies Outfitters. The elderly lady behind the counter smiled and offered assistance.

'An extra large pair of white tights, please', I requested.
'Are they for yourself, Madam ?' she asked.
'Oh yes', says I.
'Well,' said the lady, 'You won't need extra large. They would be much too big and uncomfortable.'

Sensing an argument about to develop, I said 'Oh, I don't want to wear them. I want to strain jelly through them.'

She looked at me and hastily wrapped the package of extra large white tights, accepting my money, and I equally hastily lifted the package and left the shop.

Ingenuity and improvisation came to our rescue many a time during the War and this was, for me, a personal battle. And so the crab apple jelly dripped steadily through the white tights with the legs cut off and stitched above the knee, the top bulging with the rich apple pulp. This ill-shaped jelly bag was tied to a pole suspended between two chairs back to back. The large basin on the floor collected the luscious amber coloured juices.

'And what is more, ' Heather continued, 'when I'd finished the job I washed the new-style jelly bag and gave it to Eileen next door for her boiling of the crab apples. Fortunately she just got the straining finished when the stitching gave out. There just isn't the quality in things nowadays!

Amy made it quite clear that Brandyburn had a proper jelly bag for use !

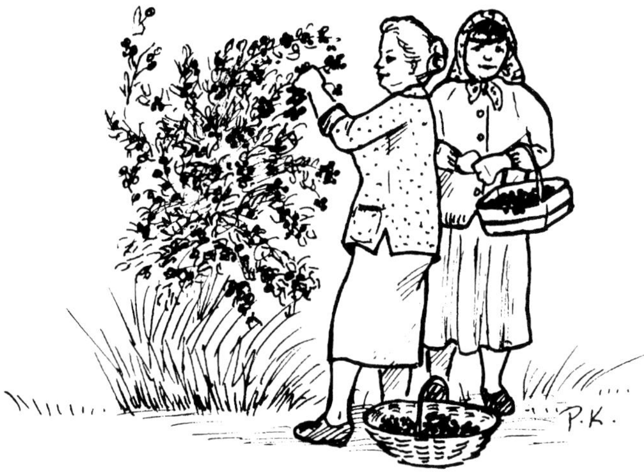
P.K.

IF I COULD TALK TO THE ANIMALS AND THEY COULD TALK TO ME

As well as our human guests we also hosted some of nature's two legged and four legged friends.

'If I could talk to the animals and they could talk to me', so said Dr. Doolittle. What could we have learned from the animals who visited us or we encountered during our time in Brandyburn?

At six-thirty a.m. a majestic full grown fox used to follow his track right round our garden patch. He would pass beneath our windows, his magnificent gold tan coat gleaming in the early morning sunshine; his brush practically sweeping the ground as he moved. Though he did stop at the compost heap, he evidently didn't find it attractive, he merely sniffed and continued on his way. Having 'marched' our boundary he left over the wall at the end of the garden to find something more enticing.

Lady guests were intrigued by the pups which next door's collie decided to produce in a warm sheltered spot under our wild bramble bushes. Yes, you were always told it was gooseberry bushes, weren't you! The ladies asked us if they could visit the maternity ward and went down the garden with tit-bits of meat and saucers of milk. No mother was better looked after.

We had plenty of fun with dogs though we didn't own one ourselves. 'Patch' a pure white collie was a lovely soft tempered animal but, after his car and tractor chasing became a dangerous obsession, he turned up one day wearing a muzzle, evidently ashamed and distressed, and nothing we could say consoled him. He never showed up again and we learned he had been put down.

A favourite successor to 'Patch' was 'Lady', the little rough-haired Jack Russell who visited every day and whom we have spoken about before. Her owners, Gerry and Mary, left home each morning to work in Clifden and didn't return till early evening. Like any other animal Lady enjoyed company so she adopted us. She was a tremendous character and if we displeased her in any way she would sit down hard on her bottom, turning her back on us. Her reaction to our asking 'Say good morning to your Aunties' was a firm upending of rear quarters for a good brisk rub. Oh, the groans of ecstasy. We mean from Lady ! When her undercarriage was dirty from crossing the boggy ground she responded to our, 'Are your feet clean?' by lying on her back, her four paws waving in the air waiting to be towel dried. She was a real comedian and we were sorry she too eventually took to chasing cars and tractors.

This behaviour was common amongst dogs in the country and a few nasty accidents happened to motorists and cyclists. We came to know the places where the dogs crouched in the long grass waiting to spring out at the unsuspecting and used to slow down and sometimes stop, a ploy they couldn't understand. If we didn't do this we just kept on going as the dogs were experts at the chasing game and could avoid us, but it was very alarming for the visitor.

The crime of mugging could take place in Clifden. During the winter, Heather had been shopping at the butchers and had bought a few slices of lamb's liver. Well pleased with all her purchases she set off to walk back to her car. On the way, she stopped to look in a shop window and was aware of a little terrier dog eyeing the plastic bag with the butcher meat. Not wishing to start an incident, Heather swung the bag over to her other hand, saying to the wee dog, 'Now, there's nothing in there for you.' The wee dog must have said to himself, 'Who is she kidding ? I know there's liver in that bag. I can smell it.' Deciding it was time to take action he followed the plastic bag and quick as a flash, stood up on his two short hind legs and neatly slit the bag with his teeth. Out fell the bag of liver, was caught just as neatly in his mouth and off he raced out of sight before Heather could wonder at what had tugged the plastic bag.

It was quite the slickest of muggings and Heather reckoned the thief deserved his spoils for such a professional job. She had to go back to the butcher, tell him she had been mugged and, please, could she have some more liver. On hearing her story Dessie, the butcher, laughed and said the dastardly deed had been undertaken by a well-known local felon !

One very unusual animal visitor was a Rhodesian Ridgeback. We spotted it walking past our kitchen window. It was so big it could practically look in to see what was cooking. Being a very warm day he lay panting in the shade so some cool fresh water was what he needed. He was very friendly and when we were later visited by Yvonne and her little girl, Zoe, he trotted after them and quite happily spent the night at their house with Yvonne's two Border Collies. The following day our friends going the mile and a half to the shops, both of them on the one bike, were followed by the Ridgeback. From our kitchen door we were laughing as Zoe sitting behind her Mummy kept turning round to look at the dog and saying, 'Pedal faster Mummy, he's still here ! '

We realised he was a pedigree animal and had been abandoned. Getting in touch with the RSPCA office (forty miles distant) they arranged to come out and collect the dog. Up to this point we hadn't quite known what breed he was, but the RSPCA representative told our friends he was a Rhodesian Ridgeback and was used as a hunting dog. He added that this animal was a very fine specimen and he knew of a good home who would gladly take him as they already owned a Ridgeback. The dog was given a gentle knock-out pill for the journey and they just managed to get him into the back of the little van before he keeled over and slept peacefully to his destination where he met up with the other Ridgeback. We like to think he has spent the rest of his life loping around with his new friend.

Ben, a white collie, was experienced at riding shotgun, standing squarely on the back of a tractor and checking all cars coming up behind them by barking furiously. How he never fell off remained a mystery and the owner often saw cars coming too close in order to take Ben's photograph. What a pity Ben couldn't wear a cowboy hat and tote a shotgun. He was a real animal character.

'Come and listen'. This came to be a frequent request from either of us as we extended our knowledge of living in the countryside. This particular evening's call was to investigate an unusual croaking sound which came from gorse bushes in the field opposite the Cottage, a weird haunting sound we couldn't identify. Luckily at this point Gerry came along on his bike and we asked the reason for the sound.

'Sure that's the corncrake. It nests out there and also in the fields near the post office.' Unfortunately with modern farming methods the corncrake has become a rather scarce bird so we were thrilled to be able to tell our bird-watching friends that, 'Yes, we still have the corncrake', as if we were personally responsible.

The cuckoo was a welcome herald of summer and called from morning till night. One guest, Yaro from Czechslovakia, had never seen a cuckoo and couldn't get enough of filming it as it sat on the telegraph wires. Sometimes its call sounded as though it was laughing at us as we slogged in the garden. Oh, the mocking ways of nature !

At the beach, flocks of curlews, lapwings, choughs, gulls and oyster-catchers were prolific. Visiting one particular bay we enjoyed the diving antics of the terns. As there were few trees for nesting, there weren't too many land birds around.

Whirring beating wings constantly stopped what we were doing to look upwards at skeins of swans flying across the sky, heads elongated forward, feet tucked underneath the huge body for all the world like the Concorde aircraft which must have had its design conceived from observation of swans. Likewise, didn't R.J. Mitchell get his idea of design for the Spitfire from lying on his back staring into the sky and studying the flight of birds?

One day we were aware of something white fluttering in a corner near our boundary wall and discovered a lovely swan in distress. It seemed to have a broken leg and all its efforts to stand and flap its wings prior to flying were being frustrated.

We could only offer pails of water from a distance, and home-going school children gave us all sorts of advice on how to deal with this 'emergency'. 'Throw it some bread' which we did but Roger, next door's spaniel, jumped over the wall and devoured the bread before the swan's neck could reach out. 'Get a net' was another instruction we ignored and knowing how strong and vicious the bird could be we dared the children to go anywhere near it.

Heather phoned the Ranger at the National Park, Letterfrack, for advice and obtained useful information on sick birds. Seemingly if the swan was not able to reach water and was doomed to die, nature would set up bacteria inside it to soften the death. The good news was that our friends Gerry and Joe were able to lift the swan and take it nearer the lake. We presumed - and hoped that with the flooded land it could move by itself to grow stronger and meet up with its feathered friends.

Another feathered visitor was a racing pigeon which landed on our roof. Where on earth did that one come from? Was he just having a rest? We never knew. A kestrel also decided to drop in and have a stroll around the concrete path at the back. Small birds, such as gold crests, tits, wrens, finches, stonechats saw themselves mirrored in our windows and got the proverbial fright when they touched the glass.

Although the countryside looked barren and grey with all the stony ground and numerous dry stone walls to enclose valuable little tracts of land to grow vegetables and hay, it was astonishing how much wild life there was around us.

Fortunately we ourselves were not troubled by rabbits, but on the beaches and dunes, the burrows honeycombed the terrain. We heard of one hunt when at night a Land Rover with headlights blazing drove across the land while the passenger armed with a shotgun did his best to control the rabbit population.

Close to the house several litters of kittens were born, each new one giving us endless pleasure as we watched their antics scrabbling to Mama cat and also finding warmth and softness in the flower tubs on the patio. When the kittens were just a few days old the Mama invariably brought them one at a time to our kitchen door to display her achievement. A particular litter was brought separately to meet us with a day between each visit. We christened them Eenie, Meenie and Miney and just hoped there would be no Mo, but there was. Mo was the tom of the litter and a right little tubby bundle. When Heather lifted him, he spat at her and stretched his claws.

Nature having its own population control meant a burial party occasionally and Amy was appointed undertaker. As she officiated, we were reminded of the hymn, 'All things bright and beautiful, all creatures great and small'. Indeed every verse of that lovely simple hymn was relevant to where we were living.

Early on in our settling in Connemara we realised a danger on the roads came not from cars or other vehicles but from animals. At that time there was little or no fencing and cows were apt to bed down on the verges and even on the tarmacadam. If the cattle were black, huddled together, and heads not visible, it was extremely difficult to see them even in the car headlights. It was only when heads up they faced the lights , the eyes and white forehead flash caught in the glare that it was easier to see them. We were told that cows were the cause of many accidents and at that time the motorist was held to be at fault. Nowadays more land is fenced off and the law has been changed making the animal owner responsible for keeping his animals under control.

When first living in the country we were annoyed to see someone dismantle a stretch of drystone wall. Was this a form of vandalism or cattle rustling Connemara style? No, it was a case of not using the field gate but, instead, take down the wall, bring out the cattle, rebuild the wall. Logic defeated us until we realised that it was common practice. Maybe saved wear and tear on the gate itself ?

Thundering down the road on many days were several Connemara ponies and everyone locally knew who they belonged to. It was a bit like the Wild West. The local Gardai were frequently called upon to have the ponies sent back to their owners. Tourists enjoyed the chaos and disruption caused by these lovely animals.

At the end of summer, groups of donkeys also took to wandering -yet again another hazard. They were looking for food from the roadside and could perhaps survive through the winter this way. On a wet day, a grey sad faced donkey looks very bedraggled.

One day we witnessed expert gamesmanship by a cow and a donkey. They had spied a solitary car, a navy blue mini parked in a large open space opposite the Craft Shop at Recess. The two passengers had visited the shop and were returning to the car. Unknown to them they were followed by the two animals. As the cow and donkey closed in on the car, we imagined the following conversation taking place.

'All right, ass. You go up to the driver's window and I'll stand in front of the car', said the large cow.

'Yes, it's my turn to cadge and hopefully eat', replied the ass. 'These two women look well fed and generous - perhaps kind to animals, maybe? I do hope they have some ham sandwiches'.

'Well,' said his pal the cow, 'they certainly can't get past me. I'll head butt that Dinky car if they try to move.'

So it was that two tourists experienced highway robbery at the Recess Craft Shop car park.

Young lambs could also prove a hazard as they liked to jump over walls in a single file following Mama. It was only efficient brakes of the vehicle which prevented the lambs finishing up in a single pile.

One day we were surprised to see a cow which was bobbing along the road like a ship at sea. The head, back and tail showed over the top of the drystone wall which bounded our garden. Going forward we realised that the cow was at the front end of a long blue rope and as the animal trotted along, wobbling from side to side in eager expectancy, the man at the other end of the rope was almost running to keep up. Surely roles were being reversed ? Normally the human leads the cow but here was the cow being master and man the servant. The man was not in the least concerned. In fact, he seemed to be enjoying his jogging. The inevitable woolly hat on his head, pullover holey at the elbow, knees of trousers caught up with binder twine, a nod of the head and we exchanged greetings - 'Soft class of a day'. In other words, 'Fine misty rain'.

We were on a new learning curve, for later in the day a noisy truck was heard trundling along and turned out to be an ancient red Ford lorry. The driver was hunched with both arms across the steering wheel intent on his driving, an old felt hat well pulled down on his head and an unlit pipe in his mouth. That was quite a normal scene, but to our astonishment riding on the float of the lorry, with only three foot high side boards to hold it in, was a horse looking very proud and handsome, mane and tail flowing out in the breeze and a wonderful glossy brown coat. Usually people go out for a ride on a horse, but here was a horse being taken out for a ride!

As we have just said this was a new learning curve beyond our com-prehension so let's put it on the Gerry list and ask him when next we see him. We did, and it was indeed, as usual, another aspect of our rural education. Gerry's little smile preceded the statement, 'Ah well, that's the stallion for the district and he's going to a mare down the Roundstone Road', adding how much the stud fee would be.

Being more bold now, we casually said, 'We suppose it is the same thing about the cow ? and, yes, the cow was desperate to get to the bull several fields away. Seemingly the bull would be too boisterous, maybe even dangerous to walk at the end of the rope to the cow in heat, whereas the stallion didn't mind keeping the mares waiting.

Some time later we learned the sequel to that particular cow when it calved. Taken into the shelter of the shed at our friend Mary's small farm the cow, after a difficult birth, slipped her calf. It was not a strong youngster and gave Mary anxious days. It didn't thrive on its mother's milk and even some aspirin dissolved in the bucket of milk Mary had taken from the cow didn't seem to work. A more drastic remedy was necessary so a drop of the ould poitin did the trick. The calf heady from its 'having drink taken' rose on its shaky, spindly legs and nuzzled the mother as if to say, 'Why did you not give me some of the fiery medicine instead of waiting for Mary?' Another first for us - meeting an alcoholic calf !

Perhaps you are more knowledgeable than us, or are quicker to see the reason for the perambulations we had witnessed for the first time of sex rearing its ugly head in Connemara !

Gradually we came to know more of nature's population of furry friends, birds of sea and land, domestic and farm animals, even the wee mouse which welcomed our first day in Brandyburn.

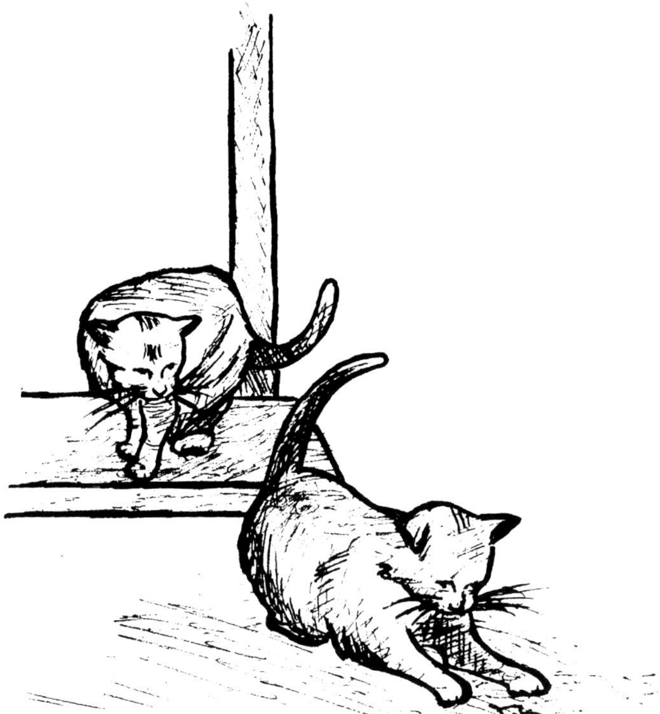
PK

CONNEMARA GOOD SAMARITANS

The road from Clifden to Brandyburn is very scenic, hugging the coastline giving wonderful views over the sea, changing at every corner. The road itself is narrow, mainly unfenced, deep ditches at each side. In summer the large volume of traffic, particularly international cars, is an added hazard with motorists entranced by the unfolding scenery tending to forget which side of the road they should be driving on.

However, that was not the reason for the dilemma facing our friends Audrey and Bobby on a winter's day. The drive from Dublin was uneventful and pleasurable and when they reached Clifden they were looking forward to arriving after their two hundred mile drive and we, knowing them very well, would have the kettle boiling for a cuppa.

Round a bend four miles from Brandyburn the setting sun, low in the sky, blinded Bobby for a moment and the car slipped off the road into a ditch. Shaken but unhurt they scrambled out, wondering what to do. They considered setting out to walk for help when, hearing the roar of an engine, they saw a car in the distance. Approaching with a screech of brakes the driver checked no-one was hurt and sympathised about their predicament. 'Never mind,' said the driver, 'we'll soon have you back on the road.' Audrey and Bobby couldn't even see an animal moving, and in view of the absence of cars and people, they were tempted to ask 'how' and 'when'. Soon another car came into view. The rescuer stepped out but on seeing two lady occupants he waved them on, assuring them everything was under control, that it was a job for a few of the lads, and thanked the ladies for offering help.

The next car was stopped and two young local men were asked 'Come and help get this man back on the road. There'll be another car along soon and we'll probably get another two to pitch in.' Sure enough, another arrived and its two occupants joined in. Before they had decided the best method, a third car arrived, stopped and the driver stuck his head out the window, saying, 'Want a tow rope?' 'Fine,' said number one rescuer, 'turn your car round and attach the rope and we'll pull yer man out backwards.'

Bobby was instructed to get in and steer when given the word, the rope would slowly take the strain and 'the lads' would take the weight, easing the car out of the ditch. In no time at all the car was back on the road, undamaged, engine ticking over and all was well. Before Audrey and Bobby realised it, the possie of cars and men rode away into the sunset and the intrepid travellers from Dublin were left wondering if they had dreamt the whole episode. 'Thanks' were not expected by the rescuers. They had just been helping fellow travellers. Good Samaritans.

Another Good Samaritan story concerned a lady from Buckinghamshire who had a holiday home half a mile down a remote track (called a boreen in Ireland) near a secluded sandy beach. An idyllic spot.

After the long journey to the ferry at Holyhead and the second long mileage from Dublin to Connemara she was happily anticipating a good cup of tea, or perhaps a gin and tonic would be more celebratory, on arrival at her holiday home. At last the moment came when she put the key in the lock but on opening the door she was horrified to find the cottage flooded from an overflowing water tank in the attic. Wearily she walked back towards the main road to find help.

She told us there were no 'locals' around but seeing a young man striding along the road she approached him. She judged him to be from a town or city because, she said, he was wearing highly polished shoes! Apparently his style was well pressed jeans with matching blue sweater and check shirt. On his back was a natty small nylon haversack in rather sober colours and along with the shiny shoes he gave the impression of the well dressed gent out in the country. Those of you who know the countryside appreciate that casual, well-worn, all-weather clothing and sturdy shoes - usually the wellies - are the familiar garb of tourist and local alike.

She smiled at him and asked, 'Are you a Good Samaritan?'

His laughing reply was, 'Well, I hope I can be considered one for I'm a Church of Ireland minister on holiday. How can I help you?'

He accompanied her along the boreen admiring the solitude of the road, the seascapes on turning corners, and the little loch they passed on the way. How, he wondered, could any transport move on such a road but was assured that an oil tanker regularly came down to deliver heating oil and hadn't tipped into the lake yet. Marvelling at all the country ways, he went into the cottage with our friend who promptly handed him a well used, and slightly unsafe, home-made ladder. Removing the haversack he scrambled into the attic with difficulty and

63

found the offending valve which was allowing the water to overflow. Switching it off his good deed was accomplished. Turning round to come down he let out a very un-minister-like shriek and made an ungainly descent from the heavens.

White-faced he looked at her and gasped, 'There are spiders up there.' Delighted that she no longer had a flood to contend with she cheerfully replied, 'Of course there are spiders up there. They're all over the place in the country. There are 'money' spiders which are small but I've never received any money because of them; and there are big hairy long legged ones which seem to live down the bath plug-hole; and the lovely ones which weave wonderful webs at windows. Oh, they're all beautiful.' Listening to this sermon he replied', That may well be but I'm very afraid of them' and grabbed his haversack from the floor which, by this time, had gathered the remnants of a cobweb his grateful hostess had brushed from his shoulders. Saying goodbye, this Good Samaritan beat a hasty retreat up the boreen to the relative safety of passing cars and lorries, grateful thanks from our friend ringing in his ears.

Working in the kitchen, we wondered what had delayed our friends, Joan and Doug from Howth for they always arrived in good time for dinner at seven o'clock. Darkness comes early in October so we were relieved when they arrived in a small noisy car which was definitely not theirs. It turned out they had had an experience similar to that of Audrey and Bobby.

Their Volvo had given trouble on the journey from Dublin and as they were running later than intended they took what they thought was a short cut across the Bog Road from near Roundstone. As its name suggests, the road is laid over the boggy ground and skirts a vast network of lochs and streams. Very scenic and not to be missed by tourists but certainly not recommended when in a hurry - and after dark.

Miles from anywhere taking a bend at an awkward angle the Volvo side-slipped landing near a large boulder. Like Bobby and Audrey, they were a bit shaken getting out of the car and taking the few steps over uneven ground to the road they had just left. Also like Audrey and Bobby they looked around, but nothing moved. Not a house light in sight. Wondering what on earth to do and how many miles would it be to 'civilisation' they heard a regular squeaking noise in the distance and out of the darkness came a man on a rusty old bike.

Glad to see him, they excitedly told him what had happened and asked would he 'phone for help. All this time, the man, cap pulled down over his eyes, unlit pipe in his mouth, well stained raincoat collar turned up to protect from the dampness of the mist, sat astride his transport, looking in disbelief from one to the other. Finally, he said he couldn't as he was in a hurry, but if they walked up the way he had just come they would see a new hotel. Delivering the information he attacked the old bicycle pedals with his tough working boots and quickly moved away, the squeaking noise fading in the mist. No Good Samaritan there, as he omitted to tell Joan and Doug that it was at least five miles to the Hotel. But perhaps he was a sort of Good Samaritan by omitting to tell them.

Before they girded themselves for their walk, car headlights appeared out of the darkness and a battered old car pulled up. Surrounded by chattering children, a smiling young woman with a cheery voice looked out and said 'How-are-ye - need any help?' Joan and Doug explained everything from slipping off the road to the advice from the dour cyclist of walking to the Hotel.

The young woman said, 'Right then. Hop in. I'll take you to your friends at Brandyburn.' With difficulty she turned the car on this narrow uneven bog road and brought them to us giving a commentary on everything all along the way. As Joan and Doug stepped back from the car, the young woman and the three youngsters waved and shouted a cheery 'Byeee' and off they went into the darkness.

Coming in the door Joan excitedly told us, 'We went off the road'. Doug, ever practical, asked 'Would you 'phone the AA to rescue the car tomorrow. It's too late tonight.'

Amy saw to their comfort, settling them down with a pick-me-up and serving their belated dinner. Joining our other guests in the sitting room for coffee Joan and Doug told their story to a sympathetic audience. From the guests many motoring experiences were related - 'my first car', 'my disastrous driving test', 'hazardous roads', 'speed traps', and now a temperamental Volvo.

Meanwhile Heather phoned to alert the Gardai, explaining that no one was hurt or lost on the bog. She was advised that the car would be better to be removed 'sooner rather than later'. Heather said that surely no one would associate the peace and tranquility of Connemara with car thieves and vandals.

'You never can tell these days, but I'll get the patrol to check it out when they are over there', was the reply.

The next call made was to Gerry when Heather asked if he could come with her to collect the luggage from the Volvo, including Joan's jewel case. On the way, Gerry lectured Heather severely never to go on the Bog Road at night: unexpected and strange happenings were associated with the lonely boglands over the centuries.

It had been a drove road used by farmers going to and from Clifden on market days. Disturbing stories and legends had been handed down through generations as to the fate of some of these people, and always the recurring phrase, 'Sometimes there are mysterious lights across the bogs'.

Reaching the Volvo, Gerry checked it wasn't damaged, decided it was a job for Mickey and his tractor and that we would go back and ask him.

'But it's nearly ten o'clock', Heather pointed out.

'That's all right. If Mickey's at home he'll be only too willing to help'.

So Mickey, a neighbour, and his son Brendan went out to retrieve the car with Gerry. After gently towing it out backwards from its boggy resting place, Gerry drove the car triumphantly to Brandyburn.

Handing the keys to Joan and Doug, they were astonished at what had been done to help them. It had all been given generously to help travellers on their way. Yet again, Good Samaritans.

This event stayed vividly in our memories : Heather being lectured by Gerry on never travelling the eight mile Bog Road alone at night and, more importantly than all that, the destination of the young woman driver with the three boisterous children would not have involved her travelling on the Bog Road. What was it Gerry had said? '… unexpected and strange happenings were associated with the lonely bog-lands.'

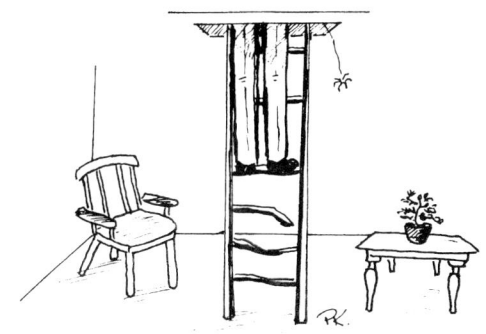

LET THERE BE LIGHT ...

Electricity poles march, sometimes at awkward angles according to wind strength, over the boggy terrain up hillsides and across lochs conveying vital power to all sorts of outlandish places. The poles seemed to disappear scattered away across the land, but in the distance lights shine out at night from unseen cottages.

Coming from the city with all mod cons we found the fairly frequent electricity failures a frustration but realised various elements caused the power cuts. Storm force winds made the cables swing alarmingly, resulting in them coming adrift from the poles, or if there was lightning in the district and it hit a transformer perhaps a large area could be plunged into darkness. Another cause could quite possibly be a swan flying into the cables and wrenching them from a pole. On these instances we were more concerned about the swan.

Contacting the local electricity office we found co-operation and rapport. Later on they were able to give advance notice of power cuts if they were expecting to work on the lines for extended periods.

During our time in Brandyburn, three linesmen lost their lives while repairing supply cables in the harsh and difficult conditions under which they worked, going out during the wildest storms. Realising the cost in human lives, we never complained of power failures.

Happily the Electricity Supply Board put into operation a long-term plan to upgrade the system and gradually the breaks in supply ceased. At the same time the telephone service was also improved by strengthening and renewing the cables which have to be very strong to withstand the severe elements in the western area.

Upgrading the electricity supply meant that some houses which had never had the benefit of electricity at last received a service.

Some months after we had established ourselves we decided to hold a garage sale of household items, such as utensils and linen which were surplus to our requirements. As many of the houses nearby were holiday homes, replacement of broken crockery, etc. was always a necessity so our sale was of use to the ladies who owned these houses. The sale was a new experience for our friends and neighbours who came along.

One item in the sale was a three-foot high vase-shaped lamp complete with shade. This item was a curiosity to some and we noticed a prospective purchaser examining it with great interest, turning away to view the rest of the goods but always coming back to the lamp. At the third examination, Amy reckoned it was time to encourage a purchase. She started a sales promotion by explaining that, if the plug wasn't the right size for the circuit, it was possible to replace it with what was necessary. Amy was dumbfoonered to be told, 'Oh, yes, I know, but you see we don't have any electricity! ' Actually our client bought the lamp! Some months later, when electricity reached her cottage, we were witnesses to the great electric switch-on and presumed 'the lamp' glowed out towards the sea. We hoped the plug was secure lest the lamp flashed like a lighthouse confusing the fishing fleet off the coast!

Another mod con which we took for granted in the city was a mains water supply. When we first arrived in Ballyconneely we were surprised to learn that not all the houses in the area were on the 'mains'.

Some of these house owners form their own co-operatives to apply for Government Grants to institute a water scheme. Even with their contributions and a Grant it is costly in terms of money and waiting times - a frustratingly long drawn out affair in most cases.

Across the road from Brandyburn is Loch Aesard which is the area's water catchment. The water is taken through the treatment plant in the pump house at the side of the loch and piped up to a giant tank on top of the nearby hill. This giant tank has replaced the much smaller one - the 'castle in the mist' which two young Americans scaled, they being our first paying guests.

The necessity for greater water capacity is an obvious sign of increased population in the district and by new houses built for locals, returned immigrants and non-Connemara-ites (if there is such a word!) wishing to have a second home.

Jack and Jill went up the hill. You know the next line - to fetch a pail of water. We had only one severe frost while in Brandyburn. Our water tanks on the roof froze solid. Off we went with buckets at the ready expecting to get a supply at the village pump a mile away. Surprise, surprise. It was also frozen solid. Two of the local council men happened along and seeing our consternation suggested a solution. 'Bring your car along the track towards the water tower on the hill, reversing it ready for going back,' we were told. Accepting this advice the hatch-back was duly opened up. To anchor the valuable cargo, the cardboard boxes which we had brought to support the motley collection of containers amazed our Sir Galahads.

Up the hill went 'Jack', a bucket in each hand, scrambling over the boulders and scree. Down he came, more cautiously, hardly spilling a drop of the water he had dipped from the supply tank after climbing the iron access ladder. The procedure was carried out a few times by this agile human goat and Brandyburn was once again serviced with that vital commodity which we and probably most people take for granted. This was one of the many illustrations of the kindness and thoughtfulness of the local people.

Carrying a bucket or buckets somewhere is not an unusual sight in the country. In the first week of our arrival we saw a man climb over the wall across the road. To us he was rather strangely dressed in a long raincoat, welly boots and a leather flying helmet complete with straps, clutching a white plastic bucket in his hand and weaving his way across the land headed up the hill. Our imagination ran riot. Could it be an illicit still he was heading for ? Could there be a house hidden up there? Oh, but the mind boggled at the possibilities. We thought up many excitingly wild plots before we found out he was going with his bucket to visit his cow for some milk. What a disappointment ! Not knowing anything about him, particularly not knowing his name, as a means of identification between us we christened him Mr. Alcock and Brown because of his flyer's helmet. (The famous fliers had landed a few miles away in 1919 and we had visited the site commemorating the event).

Being 'blow-ins' to the district we didn't know names so we 'christened' quite a few people.

Another man who cycled past our house each day was nicknamed 'the Winklepicker' - need we explain why? And, of course, his brother became 'the Winklepicker's Brother'.

We never meant this identification to be unkind or hurtful to anyone – it was a means of local identification between us.

We also had one called 'the Hitch-hiker', so named because his Sunday afternoon pastime was hitching a lift in a car, in any direction! We saw him jump out of the hedge one day, flagging down a car towing a caravan. Suddenly the road seemed to be a mass of red brake lights. Following this apparent emergency stop, the Hitch-Hiker squeezed into the back of the car which, with its caravan, continued its journey. We often wondered where he got to and how he got back! Some unsuspecting motorist would no doubt be pressed into service.

In a rural district the post van covers many miles in a day and our mail was latterly delivered by John, whom we referred to as 'John, the Post' which was a very logical nickname. When he was on holiday, a young local man took over, and earned the pseudonym of 'Deputy Dawg' when we found out he was another John. Very confusing, but we continued to refer to that John as Deputy Dawg - telling him so he was much amused.

The only nickname we knew of relating to ourselves was 'the ladies of Brandyburn' which was a nice thought considering our attempts at wo-manual labour, house painting, furniture removing and even mixing concrete! Thanks folks

SLEEPING ROUGH

We had always wanted to be Girl Guides and sleep under the stars, but never did either. Opportunity came at Brandyburn Cottage.

There were very few times when one of us gave up our room to a guest, but there was the odd occasion we agreed we did so for someone we knew well and considering their circumstances a break in Connemara would be beneficial to them.

It happened that one night both our rooms were vacated and we elected to sleep under the stars in our new sun room which was not yet finished - no lights, no curtains and certainly no street lights outside. We had two old mattresses in our utility room awaiting collection the next day so, remembering our early days in Brandyburn during refurbishing, we manhandled the mattresses to the sun room to air. It was a very warm day and they were soon toasted to perfection.

After the last guest had gone to bed we did our usual final house check and got ready ourselves. Then we encountered a small problem. The door leading from the main corridor into the porch, and then sun room, had a yale lock but no key, never had, and we didn't bother as it wasn't needed. This meant that we would have to leave the door off the latch and just hope that any guest getting up during the night didn't notice and carefully close the door. If that happened, it would mean that in the morning the elderly Girl Guides would have to come out the porch door which faced the front, run along and come in the kitchen door also at the front. The sight of the two ladies from Brandyburn in their night attire sprinting along early in the morning would have frightened the horses never mind the natives ! We dismissed this contingency but took the key of the kitchen door with us to our temporary sleeping quarters, just in case!

Looking out on the hushed land beneath a myriad of stars we were to get our wish to sleep under them. The sky had an almost midnight blue effect belying darkness. How peaceful it was until at the front of the house we could hear some of the lads walking home from the pub in the village. It sounded as if they were putting the world to rights all by themselves.

As we crawled into our make-shift beds a thought struck us. What if one of these world statesmen, feeling adventurous, decided to have a look into this new glass addition to 'The Brandyburn'. What a shock if their torch-light shone on two prostrate bodies laid out on two mattresses ! The two bodies had become hysterical by this time. However, sanity prevailed, we calmed down and spent a comfortable night like two hot-house plants.

In the morning we thankfully tip-toed down the hall and by breakfast time nobody even questioned where we had slept. Another triumph for organisational ability !

I MUST GO DOWN TO THE SEA AGAIN

The sea yields up its treasures in many ways. We had to ask a lot of questions before we understood how vital the harvest of the sea, not only fish, was for the local population.

Observing what to us looked like coal bags filled with some heavy substances we learned that they contained winkles. The children and adults carried out this back-breaking work prising the winkles and limpets from the rocks. When sufficient bags were collected and left at the entrance to their boreen, a large refrigerated container truck would come along to collect the load. Later at night it would leave with green lights shining above the driver's cab and clear lights along the top of the monster. It resembled just that – a large growling monster wending its way along the twisting road. Sometimes it did breathe smoke - blue stuff called pollution. The truck was heading to one of the Ferry ports, Rosslare or Dublin and its cargo could possibly be sold in Billingsgate, London, or another large market in the morning, even as far away as Paris. We heard that the Japanese market for shellfish was lucrative, but the local winkle pickers didn't get a great payment for all their tiring work.

Oysters and clams were another attraction to the overseas markets. They were gathered and suspended in the sea at the harbour in large 'frames' of plastic netting to await collection.

In the areas north and south of Clifden, many fish farms thrived. Mussels growing on ropes hanging from rafts floating on bobbing petrol drums were a common sight. To the eye of the true environmentalist they were ugly intrusions to the natural beauty of the inlets, but to others it meant employment and a better standard of living for families. As in other parts of the world, salmon farming is controversial but it means that the king of the fish world is now available all year round. We still say 'wild is best'.

We were fortunate to have a friend with a small boat who kept us supplied with large crab claws. He was meant to be catching the curious lobster, but the lobster wasn't always curious enough to sneak into the pot.

One very hot day our friend Gordon was dozing in his boat as it drifted in Bertraghboy Bay. Conscious of a gentle plopping noise in the water alongside, he raised himself on an elbow to peer over the edge of the boat only to come eyeball to eyeball with a curious seal. The seal dived, swam under the boat coming up on the other side to have another look at this human being. For quite a while our friend was kept amused by this sleek creature's antics.

Over the years in Connemara we looked out for the seals at their breeding grounds and watch the pups playing around in the shallow pools and endlessly climbing on and slithering off the rocks. So clumsy ashore, but so very fast and graceful in the sea.

To many of our European neighbours who visited the West, a bowl of steaming mussels was a 'must'. And what about prawns? A friend who has a small hotel hosts a large party of visiting French fishermen at the same time each year. They only want to eat fish and our friend declares that if he could produce a dessert made of fish they would want that for 'afters'.

This is beginning to sound like a cookery book, and it's no wonder fish could become an endangered species for it is so popular and excellent in health-giving properties.

The tides brought a great variety of seaweed to the shores, especially after storms. It is not an unusual sight to see two or three men in curraghs tying up very large bundles of seaweed and then joining the bundles together. At low tide a mechanical grab hauls the bundles ashore and they are then loaded on to lorries to be transported to Kilkieran for processing to a certain stage before being shipped to Scotland for further processing.

Many and varied are the end products which use the constituents of seaweed in their composition, such as soap, medicine, iodine and even at one time, glass making.

Car drivers on their sightseeing tours were surprised, but not amused, to have to sit behind a seaweed lorry oozing rich brown iodine-laden liquid, which joined the natural peaty water draining from the bogs on to the roadway giving it an opalescent gleam.

Seaweed is a very valuable fertiliser for use on the land, an important item on any farm. We learnt about this ourselves and used it generously on our garden : vegetables and flowers thrived on this bounty from the sea. Many types of seaweed are edible, for example, carragheen, usually served as a dessert and claimed to be a great health food. It was not served in Brandyburn Cottage, although we did know that some top-class hotels in Ireland had it on their menus.

RELIGIOUS OBSERVANCES

When we first moved to Brandyburn Cottage we had much to learn of local customs, some strange to us but of great significance in the life of the community. We had moved in on St. Caillin's Day which was the local Saint's Day and considered lucky.

The Stations, however, was something we had not experienced, and considered it an honour to be invited, for we are Scots Presbyterians. We learned that the history and object of holding this religious ceremony goes back many years when Church buildings were few and far between and the priest for the area would travel many miles to hold Mass in a house in one of the isolated communities. This took place once in every six months.

The chosen parishioners to host the ceremony would start preparations well before the due date. The house would be cleaned from top to bottom, the menfolk would paint and whitewash the cottage, the women bake for unknown numbers, for everyone in the area had an open invitation to attend.

In the best room an altar would be set up and when the priest arrived and had heard Confessions he would set out his chalice and relics, conducting the Mass for the assembled company.

Over our years in Ireland we realised the tremendous comfort and companionship generated by religion and Christianity in its wider sense. The Stations were a very personal and moving experience.

After Mass the hospitality of the house was given. Strong tea was favoured by the women, soft drinks for the children, stout and whiskey for the men, and of course the home baking got short shrift !

Highlight events for the children were First Communion and Confirmation. First Communion for the seven year old children was extremely important in their lives, especially those who were chosen to take a specific part in the ceremony. We felt a thrill of compassion, if that's the right word, for those innocent young people and their parents who had dressed them so carefully for their big day. The little girls in their white dresses and boys in smart suits would come and proudly show themselves off before going to church. One neighbouring boy, little Joe we called him, (Daddy Joe was one of our builders) had a special outfit and, as Daddy Joe commented, Joe had been kitted out by Louis Copland, Dublin's famous tailor ! We watched as little Joe performed his part in the ceremony and we looked across to where Daddy Joe and Mummy Eileen were sitting. The look on Daddy Joe's face was one of tremendous pride in his son and he silently mouthed the words little Joe was saying up at the altar. An obviously happy and supportive family.

Being members of the small Protestant Community in the area we attended the Church of Ireland in Clifden, though our 'own' church was sixty miles away in Galway, joint Presbyterian and Methodist in Eyre Square.

Chris-Ann died in 1982 and we were touched when Gerry, Joe and Martin offered to dig the grave at Moyard. Personal digging of graves is a mark of respect by neighbours and friends of the deceased. Hers was a very small funeral compared with that of Derek Tinne, the minister of Roundstone Church of Ireland, who had taken up the ministry after many years in the Royal Navy. We attended his funeral service and burial in the churchyard overlooking the sea. In his oration to his father, Derek's son quoted some lines from Robert Louis Stevenson's Requiem -

'Here he lies where he longed to be;
Home is the sailor, home from sea,
And the hunter home from the hill. '

Bereavements in rural villages are attended by almost everyone, including children who get their view of death in a very natural way.

It is a very emotional time . We were affected by the sadness of two funerals in successive days of a young man and a young mother who had been greatly respected for their courage in facing death, knowing they were leaving parents and children to grieve their passing.

Likewise along the nine miles which separated us from Roundstone, it was a very sad day to attend Mass of the Angels for a little child who had suffered leukemia. The villagers from all around attended, the school children filing in to the altar with posies of flowers and then filling the church with their clear voices as adults wept.

Not only did neighbours consider it an honour to dig graves but also to take turns at carrying the coffin from church to cemetery, in many cases some distance away. Their family and friends gave the oration as the priest conducted the committal service over the flower-lined grave.

On a happier note, local weddings were a time for the neighbourhood to enjoy. We ladies like to see the bride and her bridesmaids as they make their vows. In some outlying areas small bonfires are lit by the roadside to welcome the wedding cars on their journeys. Bystanders along the route are tolerant of the sounding of car horns as the wedding party and guests pass. Cattle are sometimes startled by the cacophony.

A highlight in the neighbourhood was when Bishop Cassidy came to Ballyconneely shortly after he was appointed to the Diocese of Tuam. We attended the service while our friend Yvonne helped swell the ranks of the choir.

We are Scottish Presbyterians but that didn't detract from our involvement in the life of the local community where we found welcome. The churches work in harmony and this is reflected in the attitude of everyone.

The Church of Ireland in Clifden is on the hill overlooking the bay – it is on a very exposed and windswept site. Canon Lewis also ministered to the small congregation of Moyard, 6 miles north of Clifden whose churchyard is a real haven of peace and tranquility. Visiting Chris-Ann's grave there among the spring flowers and blossoming trees in the sheltered position we appreciated Canon Lewis's suggestion of Moyard as a fitting resting place for a country woman from Fife in Scotland.

Our first Christmas morning service in Clifden was on a very cold frosty day. We sang lustility to help swell the Christmas music of the small congregation. There is no church choir since the members attending, except during the main summer holiday period, are so small but a Carol Service is held in the afternoon when members of the Catholic Church attend and their choir lead the praise.

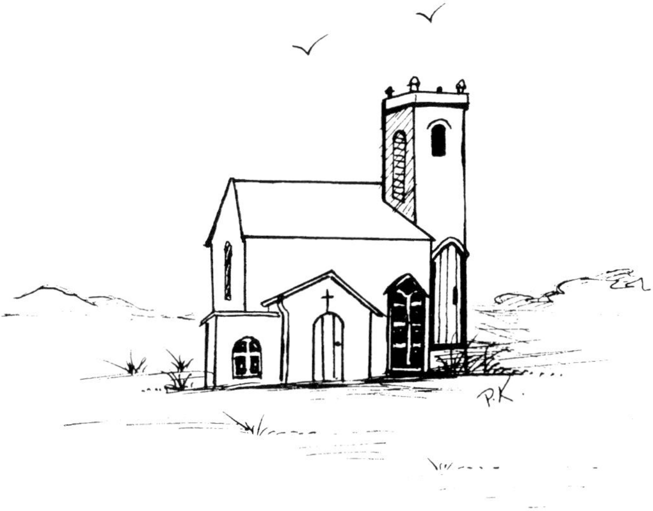
P.K.

VISITORS

Helga came to visit us from Berlin, a very long journey : plane from Berlin to Shannon, coach Shannon/Galway, service bus Galway/ Clifden, completing her journey to Brandyburn by taxi. Her English was quite good, infinitely better than our knowledge of German, but at times our conversation came to a full stop for the want of a word. At that point the gap was filled in with 'Dictionary, Helga.' After a quick word check, we were back on track again.

During our chats with Helga we established she was a Social Worker dealing mainly with disturbed young adults. Her purpose in coming to Ireland was to 'get away from it all' in the peace of the Connemara countryside and simply unwind with long walks. This she did with the result she strained her knee and had to relax for a day. We took a lunch tray to her as she sat in the garden and later when she returned the tray she exclaimed about the large meringues which had been on a plate. She had enjoyed them, 'But', she explained, 'I should not eat them. I too fat', and emphasising the statement, patted her ample tummy. 'You see', she went on, 'I should eat .... I should eat ....' and was at a loss for the right word. Ignoring the necessity of the dictionary she laughed heartily saying, 'I should eat ...' another pause, and putting her hands on her shoulders flapped her arms up and down saying, 'Cock-a-doodle-doo'! We liked Helga very much.

After her week with us, Helga planned to travel onwards to Inishbofin Island which lies some miles off the coast at Cleggan, north of Clifden. It surprised us that Helga should know of this island, but she explained that in her research of 'trying to get away from it all' she had discovered Inishbofin on the map and so had booked herself into a Guest House there.

The day before she was due to leave Brandyburn she came to us with the request, 'Please, find out from the Captain what time the ship she swims.' We knew what she meant and phoned Cleggan to check what time Paddy left Cleggan pier with passengers and goods to go to 'Bofin. 'The ship' was, and to the best of our present knowledge still is, a sturdy fishing boat, both Paddy and boat well suited and skilled in tackling the ever changing Atlantic seas around the County Galway coastline. It is not uncommon for visitors to be unable to return to the mainland until the angry seas calm down a bit.

On the morning of Helga's departure she spent more time than she should have in saying her goodbyes to fellow guests and Amy. Heather meanwhile was standing at the front door with the car engine ticking over, ready for a quick get-away to take Helga to Clifden to catch the service bus for Cleggan. In spite of 'putting her foot down' they arrived at Clifden to find the bus had already gone. They had no option but to chase along the bus route, but there was no sign of the bus. It turned out it was the day the driver takes an alternative route. Not knowing this, Heather had arrived in Cleggan before the bus ! To add to the confusion, on the run down into Cleggan Rosie, the Fiesta, started bunny jumps. When it finally limped into the parking area, it refused to start again. Saying goodbye to Helga at the ticket office, Heather returned to the car just in case it had changed its mind, but no, Rosie wouldn't budge. A telephone kiosk, mercifully one which worked, was found. A quick call to Amy told her of the impending return being delayed, then another call to Gerry O'Malley our garage guru, explaining the problem. Making a telephone diagnosis of flooded plugs he said, 'Don't worry, I'll be with you within the hour'.

Automobiles are wonderful inventions until they start to go wrong !

Meanwhile, back at the house, Heather's dilemma produced one for Amy. An elderly lady guest without a car, needed to get the daily bus to Galway as it passed through Ballyconneely and she could then catch her train to Dublin. Nothing for it but Amy had to load the lady and her luggage, taking them the mile to the village, and waiting till the bus arrived to see all safely on board.

Two guests who had arrived in the Dining Room received a surprise that morning - they had to cook their own breakfast when the time came. They took this unexpected turn of events in good part and, they told us, enjoyed the experience !

Another interesting young visitor was Elsa from Stockholm. As in the case of Helga, she had written to make a reservation and gave us a note of her arrival time by bus in Clifden. Amy met the bus. She was delighted to welcome the young woman who had long light auburn hair under a floppy black beret, a corded jacket over a long flowing black skirt, under which peeped strong, sensible black walking shoes. The crowning touch was a wonderful carpet bag clutched in her hand. Could it be that Mary Poppins had come to life ?

After her long journey Elsa retired early to bed but next morning enquired about renting a bike. She spent the short time with us speeding along the country roads with her long black skirt and long hair flowing in the breeze. The combination of the breeze and clear sunlight gave her a bad attack of sunburn on her nose and the back of her hands, but still she pedalled on. We supplied plenty sun tan cream which was soothing even though she was a bit late in its application. People don't realise the strength of the rays in the clear unpolluted atmosphere of the west of Ireland.

Elsa wanted to see as much of the district as possible and before coming had read a book in Stockholm about the abject poverty in Ireland and people with dilapidated housing. In her travels from Shannon she could hardly believe the sight of the modern houses, some resembling Spanish haciendas, the well-fed inhabitants and such healthy and happy children skylarking around and wearing shoes, something else she had not expected. We did discover that the book in question had been written in the early 1950s.

We asked why she had chosen to come all the way to Connemara and she replied that on looking at the map it appeared to be the most westerly point of Europe. She planned her annual holidays by having a relaxing country-style trip one year and alternated with visits to the New Orleans Jazz Festival. It surely couldn't have been a bigger contrast.

Every night Elsa stunned us by coming into dinner in yet another long black skirt, an immaculate white high-necked long sleeve blouse and her hair piled high on her head, clasped by a black velvet bow, every inch a most glamorous model. There must have been some magic in her carpet bag.

It was always pleasant to receive a letter from far afield, making reservations. One such came from Milan and later the young couple came to stay, driving from Milan through Europe, a ferry to Rosslare in the south of Ireland and touring from there to reach Ballyconneely. We thought them very adventurous. They too rented bikes for a day, as they said, 'To get the feel of the countryside at a more leisurely pace'.

A couple wrote from Annapolis, Maryland, USA. We presumed they would arrive by rented car from Shannon. You can imagine our astonishment when early in the afternoon of an extremely wet day a bedraggled pair of walkers landed on the doorstep.

Giving them an Irish Cead Mile Failte we commiserated with them as they shrugged off their backpacks. Noting their sodden state we suggested hot baths as first priorities. Grateful thanks from Jim who was wincing, explaining his thick woollen socks were sticking to his blistered feet! Foot salve cream to the rescue.

Tea and sympathy followed round the turf fire in the sitting room when we heard the story of their Irish holiday. Some years before, Jim and Jan had done a whirlwind tour of Ireland with their young family, this with a view to the two of them doing a walking trip in their retirement after they had decided which part of the tour had impressed them most. County Galway, and Connemara in particular, had been their choice and they made plans. Flying to Shannon, they hired a car for a couple of days to explore County Clare and the area between the airport and Galway city. Then they began the sixty mile walk to Clifden.

They were very enthusiastic about all they had seen on their way to us : the majesty of the mountains, the peaty brown little lochs, the ever-changing colour and light, the friendliness of the people they met and even the curiosity of the cattle by the wayside.

Amy was going to Bunowen Harbour for fish for the evening dinner. Jim and Jan accepted her offer of the drive and indeed we were able to give them a mini-Cook's tour of lanes, boreens, seascapes at Aillebrack. The golf course interested them both for they played golf in Annapolis, but there was no time to try out the course on their short stay.

Their walking route was to finish at Clifden, stay overnight there, then get a service bus to Galway en route Shannon. After their night with us we took them to Clifden, checked them in to a friend's guest house where they left the backpacks and were able to move about unencumbered to see as much as possible of Clifden and its coastline. We recommended they should definitely climb the Sky Road.

One year, early in May, a young American stopped and enquired for accommodation with the request that he would need breakfast early.

'No problem', we said, 'what time?'

'No later than seven o'clock, ladies, for I am having a round of golf and then I have to dash back to Shannon to meet my wife. She prefers to come a day later than me - she can't stand golf'.

Early breakfasts were not the norm in Ireland, most holiday-makers lying in bed as long as possible, some not even managing to surface till 10 a.m., though to be fair they made the most of the evening hours with entertainment in hotels and pubs. The night life in Ireland is world renowned.

Dressed to kill rather like the professional player on the major Open Competitions, our golfer was early for breakfast and studying the scorecard we had given him to check lengths and pars - he liked the descriptions of the holes.

We wondered had he managed to tear himself away from the course and speed south to meet his wife on time.

Next year the same thing happened. We were working in the garden and on hearing a car crunch on the gravel Amy went to investigate. She was back in a minute, all smiles, with our American.

'Hi', said Heather. 'Were you in time to meet your wife?'

'Oh, you remember me?' the young man said laughing.

'Could we forget you!' came the chorus.

'Is it golf tomorrow morning then?' Amy asked.

'No. This time I plan on walking up Croagh Patrick at Westport. Could I have my breakfast early, please?'

We never did find out if he was able to make his climb and get back to meet his wife at Shannon Airport the second time. Perhaps after that visit she gave up on crazy Irish holidays.

A lasting pleasure for us must be all the happy memories we have of our guests who arrived as strangers and left as friends.

THE LANDLADIES' HOLIDAY

At the end of 1982, a trip to the States was planned which would last ten weeks. A holiday for the seaside landladies could only be taken 'out of season' and so we flew from Dublin to New York via Shannon in mid November. At first sight perhaps November doesn't seem the best time of year to go holidaying, but as everything was to be so new and different it didn't appear an unusual time of year to us.

The plane was an Aer Lingus jumbo jet and seemed to cater for all ages. A young mother with a baby and a toddler was seated across the passage, the toddler having plenty fond attention from the hostesses and lapping it up as if it was all an everyday event. Perhaps it was - their destination was Shannon!

After touching down at Shannon Airport, we indulged in Duty Free shopping and as we returned to our seats we spoke with the Senior Hostess standing at the cabin door.

'Do we fly over Connemara on the outward flight route?' we asked.

'Yes,' she replied. 'What part are you wanting to identify?'

'Ballyconneely, where we live, but as it's a very small village Clifden the capital would be more of a possibility to pick out.'

'Ballyconneely,' she repeated with a smile. 'I know it well. My uncle has a shop in Clifden and I often visit there. I'm afraid we cross the coast too far south to identify any place in Connemara.'

Over the years as we sat in our sunroom at breakfast and saw the transatlantic flights cleaving the early morning sky heading for Shannon, we remembered our flights.

Approaching New York, a young Irish man sitting beside us told us he was returning to his job there and enjoyed living in New York. He pointed out landmarks and districts around the city as we circled prior to landing.

Once all the airport formalities were completed and luggage collected, we travelled by Airport coach and taxi to the city centre and checked in at our Hotel. We had arrived in the heart of the Big Apple and the Algonquin Hotel ! This proved a good choice - it was very central, one of the older hotels and a mecca over the years for many literary giants. The Irish writer Brendan Behan had been a frequent visitor.

The adrenalin was pumping away, jet lag was forgotten and we didn't feel like going to bed. In spite of being endlessly fed on the plane, accompanied by a film and cat napping was the best we could manage in the sleep department, we craved a simple sandwich and tea. In best posh-hotel style we rang down for Room Service, but the mistake was in asking for a club sandwich and, yes, you know what's coming. About ten minutes after the order was placed, there was a knock at the door and a young man, immaculate in waiter's white jacket pushed in a trolley covered in a sparkling white cloth with large hotel plate cover sitting in the middle, tea pot, cups and saucers, damask table napkins and a crystal vase sporting two pink carnations. We immediately protested that there must be some mistake as we had only ordered a sandwich. 'Yes, ladies', replied the young man and, with a flourish, removed the plate cover and there sat two club sandwiches like miniature Empire State Buildings. Wooops - our mistake!

The waiter proceeded to raise the sides of the trolley and set it up, chatting away asking where we had come from and when we said Ireland, he told us he came from County Meath and was working in New York to make enough money to go home, build a house and get married. He spoke of his good working conditions in the Hotel and social life in the Big Apple with Irish friends, but made it clear that Ireland was home and he hoped to be in a position to return soon. So the first conversation with a 'local' New Yorker turned out to be a young Irishman !

Relaxing over our 'snack' we had the pleasant surprise of receiving a basket of fruit sent up to the room with the compliments of the Management.

The conversation with the young man still in our minds, our thoughts turned back to Ireland and to Brandyburn. Before we left we had asked that patient fellow Gerry to build on a sun room at the western end of the Cottage. Just like that ! Not at all surprised, he put the heel of his boot to good use in marking out the boundary of this extension on the loose sand and gravel. From the ground a low wall would be built and then double glazing would take over above it. The entry would be from the porch already there. That was the basic requirement and, knowing Gerry by this time, we knew we could leave it to him. Having just left Brandyburn three days before, here we were wondering if it was finished ! Fortunately at that point sleep overcame us.

Taking advantage of staying in the city centre we set out on foot to see the sights. At Brandyburn there was space all around us and lots of sky. In New York we had to look for the sky around the top of the skyscrapers. Each morning we had breakfast in the Cafe next to the hotel, our friends who had made the reservations advising us to do this to meet the real New Yorkers, and we did. We were fascinated by the number of people who came in to a high counter, waited a few minutes, then clutching a brown paper bag went out again. If only we knew what was in the bag ! The staff who served us were friendly and wanted to know where we came from. By the end of the four days they immediately greeted us as we arrived.

It is nice to meet business contacts in their home environment, so we were pleased to accept an invitation to visit Ilona in her New York apartment. Ilona came to Ireland and Europe in her capacity as a scientist, and over the years we had enjoyed her friendship. In films and books, New York apartments seemed glamorous : we were not disappointed.

However, we were overwhelmed by her kindness in giving us a cheque to choose a gift in Maceys as she, now being elderly, had not been able to shop for it herself.

Before leaving for the States, a friend of Heather's suggested, if we had time, we call in on her son, Patrick, who had been seconded to the New York branch of an Irish bank. We were happy to do this and were delighted when he took us to experience a typical 'brown-bag' lunch as in our few days in the city it seemed as though every New Yorker clutched a brown paper bag at almost every hour of the day. At last we knew what could be in the bags coming out of the Cafe and for what reason - breakfast, elevenses or lunch.

During our lunch date, it was interesting to hear of his temporary sojourn in the city as he appreciated all the opportunities presented to him, by the Bank, but a return to Ireland was his eventual goal.

Being tourists in New York we had decided to do 'all' the tourist things so booked a city coach tour. So many place names came to life for us : Wall Street, Harlem, Central Park, St. Patrick's Cathedral, the Rockefeller Centre, Manhatten, etc. So many sights as well as visiting shops known to us by name only, such as Saks, Tiffanys and Maceys were visited. We 'did' them all, but spent very little ! Eventually we returned to the Algonquin, heads reeling with all these new experiences. Ah, New York, New York !

From New York, Ohio was the next stop to stay with Amy's friends, Eleanor and Fritz. They were so hospitable and nearly proved the old adage 'to kill with kindness'. On our visit, Eleanor and Fritz wondered what to show us in the month of November. The fields were bare having been harvested, the days were short, the winter had come, Christmas decorations were being anchored firmly in the streets of Haskins, the River Maumee would freeze over they told us and would start to thaw in the spring with an awesome crash of ice breaking.

We were introduced to many of their friends and one family we visited, the Winnigs, were heavily involved in farming. The countryside where they live is very flat - huge fields seemingly without boundaries carry the eye across the landscape. Betty Winnig had invited us to lunch and all the food placed on the table had been 'grown' on the farm with the exception of marshmallows. Pride of place on the table was the centrepiece - a small round tray holding Irish souvenirs she had collected when attending an International Meeting of Country women. She was very proud when her lunch guests remarked on the various objects and excitedly told us the story behind each purchase.

After lunch, son Gordon, aged twenty-two, was directed to show us something of the farming activities. Firstly to the very modern hygienic pig breeding houses where the little pink bodies enjoyed 'The Good Life', summer and winter.

He explained how the fields for miles around grew Indian maize and tomatoes and, showing us a group of shacks explained that migrant workers were necessary to descend en masse at harvest time to complete the job, time being of the essence. The tomatoes were grown small and rock hard and conveyed into huge hoppers. 'Don't they get bashed and squashed ?' we asked.

'No,' he said. 'They must be harvested like that. The processing by one of the world's best known makers of canned tomato soup does the rest.'

Taking us to see the machinery used for various activities we were astonished at the computer-operated mechanisms for ploughing, sowing, reaping and mowing. From our five foot plus heights, which did not even reach the top of the wheel hub of one gigantic piece of equipment, we eventually managed to scramble up into the driving seat. It was like being atop a sky-scraper.

Gordon asked what sort of tractors we had in Ireland. Taking us to a huge hanger-like shed we traversed in front of a range of machinery, all colours and sizes. 'No', we said as we passed each one, 'in our part of Ireland the tractors are much smaller by comparison.'

Along with all this obvious modern mechanisation, the Winnigs were hard workers and displayed all the signs of a closely committed family. For us, it was an unforgettable visit in every way.

Flying from Detroit to Baltimore in Maryland, our next destination was to visit Alice and her husband Gene in Monkton. This was a first actual meeting for the schooldays' pen pals, Heather and Alice. But how easy it was for the two of them - no problem of International communication. It was strange to think that we had their daughter Teener and her husband Ray visit us at Ballyconneely on their honeymoon the previous year, and now at last her mother and Heather were meeting.

Walking the land around Gene and Alice's home we saw, for the first time, some beautiful bright red birds on the hedges. This was our introduction to the red cardinal - a bird we had only seen on American Christmas cards. Another we later saw for the first time when visiting Alice's sister, Ruth, in Baltimore was a blue jay. This again was another colourful bird, sharp of eye and about the size of our blackbird, the red cardinal being slightly smaller. Ruth told us she had a large variety of feathered visitors to her bird table who occasionally set a marauding squirrel running for safety. Some days later when we were on our way to visit Teener in Pennsylvania, we were to witness the arrival of flocks of Canada geese which left the field shimmering to the eye - and noisy too.

Thanksgiving Day was the day after we arrived in Maryland and an invitation to a Thanksgiving Party awaited us. We were to join Alice and Gene at her nephew Pete's home on Chesapeake Bay with other members of the family. Our first taste of such a celebration displayed a close-knit family celebrating an old tradition and paying us the compliment of inclusion. The whole family adopted us and showed such warm hospitality. It was a real pleasure for Heather to meet them as they had just been names for many years.

The meal was typical of the day and along with all the goodies we had our first taste of pumpkin pie and also pecan pie. They are favourites with us to the present day.

With Alice we visited Annapolis - such a lovely city - dominated by the U.S. Naval Academy. Remembering our walking friends, Jim and Jan of the blistered feet who visited Brandyburn, we tried to telephone them to say 'Hi' but were unsuccessful. When leaving Brandyburn they had left their phone number in Annapolis urging 'If you are over in the States, get in touch'. It was disappointing not to make contact, but perhaps they were off walking somewhere!

On one of our strolls around the boundary of Gene's field a pony grazing there eyed us with some disinterest but eventually came to us. He was probably wondering where his young rider was. Alice's other daughter Alou and husband Steve lived next door and this was son Conor's pony. His sister Alison was still too young to ride and the sport was definitely out for the new baby, Andrew.

We spent happy sunny hours out in the garden with these lovely friends in Monkton whose countryside reminded us of parts of County Kildare, verdant fields grazing horses. We had the pleasure of attending a Meet with the participants suitably dressed for the Hunt. It was all just like home.

At the end of our visit to Maryland, Gene and Alice kindly drove us to Washington where we met up with our friends from Florida, Dorothy and Marie, who had given her name to the 'creek' in Brandyburn garden ! In their company we embarked on the sights of Washington, including the White House. We didn't see you-know-who but nevertheless enjoyed our two days in Washington visiting all well-known sights. We found Arlington Cemetery in the fading light of a November afternoon a most emotional experience.

On the road again with Dorothy driving, we headed south and stopped for two nights in Colonial Williamsburg which we found fascinating, a place of great character. On the way again, we spent a few hours in Savannah, Georgia, where walking along the Quay we spotted a familiar flag on an Irish registered cargo ship. Just like walking along by the Liffey, we thought !

After three days driving we reached Jensen Beach in Florida where we spent some happy weeks with Dorothy, Marie and their many friends as well as lapping up the sunshine.

As we moved in our travels we constantly met people who had great empathy with anything Irish and of course a great many Americans with Irish connections and family 'back in the old country'.

A near embarrassing situation occurred at Disney World where we were experiencing the Four Day Tourist Visit with Dorothy and Marie. We had gone with them to Mass on Sunday which at that time was held in one of the large Hotels, the Contemporary, as there was no church within the Disney World complex. The young priest was welcoming everyone and endeavouring to discover from which part of the world they all came. When he asked if there was anyone from Ireland, the two seaside landladies shouted 'yes'. In response to that we received a round of applause from the congregation and pats on the back from nearby worshippers telling where their mothers, fathers, grand-parents had come from. We were a bit shy of saying too much in case someone picked up the Scots accent and the illusion was shattered!

Our visit to America was a never to be forgotten trip. We had covered many miles from New York to Ohio, to Maryland, across to Pennsylvania, to Washington, to Williamsburg and down the long route to Florida, visiting Cape Kennedy Space Centre whilst at Disney World. We had met many Americans in their homes, been given generous hospitality, learned of their traditions and crafts.

Throughout our tour we experienced much kindness from our friends and their friends. We were interested in the lovely food put before us and always enquired about it. When the conversation ended we were asked if we would like the recipe and of course we always said 'Yes please'. We had to stop this practice very tactfully as we found it wasn't just the recipe, but the recipe books which were given to us and our luggage was getting heavier after each visit ! We appreciated this generosity but it was getting out of hand for us, no pun intended.

We had learned a little of their cooking and in hotels and restaurants seen the presentation of food in all its aspects and wondered if this education could be adapted to Brandyburn. It probably couldn't our situations were poles apart.

Following this trip to the States, we were to receive phone calls from America making reservations to stay with us. The telephone calls always started, 'Hi! I'm phoning from the States and your friends told me to call and book to stay with you when we're touring Ireland'.

The world isn't such a big place after all.

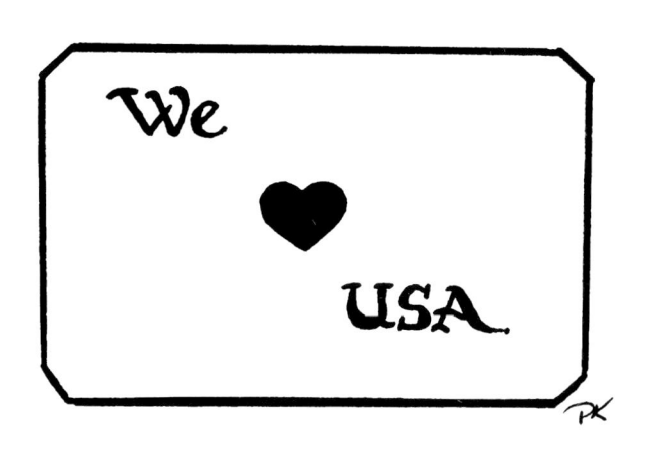

CONVERSATION PIECES

Relaxing in the Sitting Room after dinner with our guests, can you imagine the range of conversations which lightened those evening hours and made for a very happy household?

Visitors had a notion that to own a turf bog was somehow romantic and would ask, 'Do you have a turf bog?'

Our reply was, 'Unfortunately no, although we would have liked to be able to brag that we had'.

We explained that usually in April men leave their homes in the morning, riding bicycles, or on foot, heading for their turf bog. It is an annual ritual to delve the slaine, the implement for cutting, into the matted brown ground. Following the cutting, successive stages of drying have to be done. Eventually, after the final 'footing' has been completed the turf sods have to be taken quite long distances to the nearest point on the bog road. From there the turf is loaded on tractors and trailers and brought home. Even then the job is not finished for the turf has to be properly skibbled into a stack at the side of the house. Such skibbling is a work of art for it is essential that rain is deflected from the stack and the inner core of sods kept dry ready for burning in the fire or range. The whole business of turf cutting and hauling is a hard job.

The entire family plays its part in this essential task going to the bog area by bicycle or walking, and joining the man of the house when it's time to eat. A lazy curl of smoke comes up from the bog and the kettle is soon boiling. Sandwiches are passed round and a very welcome rest is taken from the back-breaking job. After the meal, the family start to help with the footing and, with good humour and groans, the combined effort makes the job seem easier.

Turf cutting has its problems in warm humid weather. We remember John the Post telling us how he, his family and the other turf cutters were chased off the bog by clouds of stinging midgies. Not even pipe smoke, cigarette smoke or turf smoke deterred the wee beasties in their persistent attacks.

Before we took over Brandyburn we arranged for a load of turf to be delivered but were mesmerised when asked if we wanted it skibbled. 'Yes', we said, not knowing what skibbled meant and hoping that our ignorance didn't show. Whatever way the turf was delivered we just presumed we could cope with it. This was to be one of the first country expressions we learned.

Later on, another of our ignorances came to light. There were, perhaps still are, quite large tracts of land in Ireland which are designated commonage with several people having the right to graze their sheep and cattle.

One such was almost opposite our house. One day we watched anxiously as people armed with clipboards and measuring tapes crossed the land. Was this some building development we wondered? Eventually we discovered that the Land Commission had agreed to divide up the land so that by drawing lots, the seventeen or so people who had the right to graze could have their own measured portion in outright possession. Such was it then that we increased our interpretation of the word 'striping', for this process of dividing the land was called 'striping the commonage'.

Another misnomer to our mind was 'opening a drain'. We thought Mary, our friend of the alcoholic calf, was a strong woman to 'open a drain' for we envisaged her lifting a three foot diameter iron, drain cover as in the city, whereas Mary was talking about a neighbour digging a ditch for her to drain surplus water away from her land.

Such local customs were an education to our guests as they had been to us.

We were fortunate to have the setting summer sun shed a luminous deep pink glow over the sitting room. New arrivals joined us and our other guests for coffee and exchange of chat about what everyone had done and seen during the day. Stories developed and sometimes an interlude of light classical music was played by one of the guests. The 'token' wit told his jokes - all very harmless. The hours were passed in congenial pleasure.

An English lady staying with us kept jumping up to go to the window with her newspaper and we were all intrigued as to the reason. Not backward at coming forward, we asked ! She told us she was fascinated at the extent of daylight and was trying to see how late she could read her newspaper by natural light.

A couple who came from Texas were completely bowled over by the ever-changing spectrum of colours ranging from clear blues to green, to browns and to purples which apparently was something they didn't experience in their part of Texas. Especially to city dwellers who hardly ever had the opportunity to see this panoramic splendour, the changing mood of the skies was a wonder. Like children, we mentally clocked up that Ballyconneely is better than Texas!

As Mother Nature has a hand in everything, we sometimes thought that our guests were equally colourful and changeable in mood. Some arrived tired after the two hundred mile journey from Dublin, some perhaps ready for a rest after a stressful time, some arriving after a long-haul flight from the States and then a drive to Brandyburn.

Within twenty-four hours the signs of stress and weariness had gone – the slower pace of Connemara had taken over.

The word 'colourful' brings to mind a couple who visited for the first time - we shall call them Mr. and Mrs. X - and joined our other guests in the Sitting Room in the late evening. They explained that their daughter, her husband and four young children had rented a house but felt that twenty-four hour contact with the family could be a bit much for Gran and Grandpa in their seventies, so daughter had booked them in with us for bed and breakfast. The other guests agreed wholeheartedly, grandchildren were great in small doses but as people get older the exuberance of children in the early hours of the morning was more than one could cope with.

Mr. and Mrs. X expressed delight with the atmosphere of Brandyburn, their very first visit to a Guest House. 'Just like a small house party' was the parting comment as they set off for bed.

Next morning when Heather was serving breakfast to the assembled guests, the glass panelled dining room door opened to admit the couple. All eyes turned to them and happy 'Good mornings! were exchanged. Mrs. X made her entrance. Bouffant hairdo, necklace of diamonds, rings of emeralds, pink quilted satin dressing gown, silver bedroom slippers and to complete the outfit, leather handbag carefully swinging from her arm. Mr. X was equally dapper. Hair carefully brushed, moustache clipped, cravat with gold pin at the neck of his blue brocade dressing jacket over pyjama trousers of wide red and blue stripes. Leather moccasin slippers completed his picture. They did not seem to notice that the other guests were casually dressed in outdoor attire, some for golf, others for a day's driving and sightseeing or just walking the beach.

It was like a scene from a Noel Coward play caught in a freeze frame. If only there had been a brief chorus of 'Some day I'll find you ....'

Amy was fortunate enough to see them when they had finished breakfast, and we affectionately christened them between ourselves 'Noel and Gertie'. Some years later we saw the stage play of that name in London and had to choke back our laughter as we remembered our 'Noel and Gertie'.

'It must be fascinating to have paying guests from so many different places' was a familiar comment in the sitting room. And, yes, we did find it stimulating and rewarding to share in the undoubted talents people have - if you have time and opportunity to hear of them.

Discretion meant we couldn't be too free with information on guests but we could indicate some aspects of the variety of people we came to know.

One guest confided to those in the sitting room one evening, 'Do you remember when Maureen O'Hara was running across the field with her red hair streaming out in the breeze in The Quiet Man?' she asked. 'Well, that was me.'

London featured in conversations for we had enjoyed the discretion of a nanny to aristocratic babies and a lady who was on Prince Charles household staff at Buckingham Palace. She testified to his natural courtesy and greatly admired the atmosphere in the Palace.

Seeking the quiet life at different times was an ambassador and also a Government Minister with his wife. They enjoyed the informality of the guest house and were able to relax from their arduous duties in the peace of Connemara.

We have all heard of the judiciary and system of Assizes in England. The visiting Circuit Judges sometimes had to spend many days even months during periods of Trials. Hotels were not an answer so certain Crown Residences were at their disposal to ensure a high degree of security. One lady guest was Housekeeper at such a Residence.

It was strange how certain years seemed to attract the same professions or interests. Not all at the same time we would hasten to add. For example, one year we seemed to have musicians and of course we and our other guests benefitted from them. A young married couple were members of the Basle Symphony Orchestra; a lady Professor at the Paris Conservatoire delighted us with short after-dinner recitals of Chopin, Liszt, etc.; Rudi was a jazz pianist; Oliver a clarinetist and we had some light operatic singing from the Shows; Gilbert and Sullivan inevitably got 'big licks'.

Another year we had psychologists - clinical, educational, occupational, and also a famous neurologist from the States, not forgetting medical doctors.

Being only four miles away from the renowned Kenneth Webb painting studio we had guests attending his Courses and sometimes we were fortunate enough to see some of their work depicting the Bog Road, seashore and village landscapes. We found it difficult to understand the resulting canvasses of those who worked in the abstract form, but the painters were very kind to us - they did not consider us complete visual illiterates ! We did find it fascinating to note they could see pinks and blues in what to us were only black turf bogs.

The Church was represented by delightful nuns from Ireland and abroad. Father John from San Diego, interested in all sorts of computerised gadgets, gave us advice on them (alas unheeded). We had always to remember to cook his breakfast eggs 'easy and over' and purchase a bottle of tomato sauce. Canon Wood, with his Scrabble, and his humorous poem naming all the guests during his stay, was a real live-wire and we always enjoyed his visits with his wife Oonagh. From the denominations of Presbyterian, Anglican, Baptist, Churches of Scotland and Ireland came ministers and bishops with wives where appropriate. Academia was represented by lecturers and professors from various Colleges and Universities.

Young Hugh, aged 12, fancied himself as a fisherman. He came armed with new fishing rod and had been given sage advice from his friends in Dublin that to get bait you watered the ground and the worms would come to the surface. We were just grateful he didn't know that the seagulls stamp on the ground rather like doing an Indian war dance and the worm pops his head out to see who's knocking at his door !

We had been surprised that we had very few worms in our garden and had been absolutely ecstatic when we got loads of manure which contained hundreds of hard working worms.

Anyway, Hugh did try to get worms but not very many gave themselves up so he begged some crusts of bread and any scraps we could offer. Not wishing to dampen his enthusiasm, first Heather and then Amy volunteered to go with him after dinner on two successive nights and try his hand at 'the fishin'. The first expedition was to a small lake on the Bog Road. Casting first with worms and then with bits of bread and bacon, it was a disappointed Hugh who had to admit defeat after an hour in the cooling breeze which was sweeping the countryside.

As so often happened, our four-legged friend, Lady, went with them on the fishin' but quickly became bored at the absence of action. There aren't many rabbits to chase by the lakeside and many a look of sheer boredom was transmitted to the two minders.

Next evening it was to another larger lake, a favourite with visiting fishermen. Perhaps this would be better. Again worms, bread crusts and scraps of fat from lamb cutlets did not produce a thing.

We had decided that Hugh would not disappoint his parents who had gone visiting some friends also holidaying in the area. During the day when collecting fish at John Roberts' Fishery at Bunowen Harbour, we had purchased a plaice and conspiratorily with Hugh after his abortive fishing expedition, rested the fish on a platter with a large printed card –

> 'Plaice   ….   weight   ….   lbs
> Caught at Lough Easard by Hugh.
> First prize for a novice. '

The platter was left on a small table near the bedroom occupied by Mum and Dad who returned after midnight by which time our fisherman was fast asleep. A note was also left for them to put it in the kitchen fridge before going to bed !

Mum and Dad had a good laugh and congratulated the fisherman at breakfast, but teased Amy and Heather about catching a sea water fish in a fresh water lake ! The other guests who had been let into the platter joke had quickly moulded a Challenge Cup from a vase and silver foil begged from the kitchen and presented it to Hugh.

Tommy, Ita and Hugh left us for a visit to their own mobile home in County Roscommon and, naturally, the fish went with them. When they arrived there late afternoon it was placed (sorry about that pun) in the fridge. Very early next morning Tommy was awakened by young Hugh begging him to light the Calor Gas Cooker so that he could have his fish grilled for breakfast. Never was a fish handled with such tender, loving care !

Before leaving for Roscommon, Tommy and Ita remarked on the quality of vegetables they had had. Tommy added, laughing, 'Particularly the potatoes!', and asked if we got them locally. We explained that while we had hopes of being self sufficient in our vegetable growing, we had soon realised our optimism was not well founded. Fortunately we made a true friend in Kevin Stanley of Clifden who agreed to supply us from his interesting market garden.

This was a real joy for it was more than merely telephoning our order the night before to collect the freshly harvested produce early next day. We had environmental and philosophical discussions, we learning so much more of the plusses and minuses of working with the elements of Connemara.

Unusual herbs were in Kevin's garden and we benefitted from their versatility and also enjoyed using the edible flowers of that wonderful deep blue of borage and the yellow trumpets of courgette blooms.

Oh, how our guests drooled at the asparagus spears dripping Kerrygold !

Salad vegetables were varied. Root vegetables freshly prised from the rich brown soil tasted so different from plastic wrapped supermarket offerings. Cabbage, cauliflower and broccoli families were especially welcomed at table and Kevin introduced us to scrumptiously tender greenish white whorls of calabrese. Even today calabrese is hard to come by in the U.K.

Returning from collecting our order we sniffed the earthy freshness of Kevin's veggies and knew we couldn't compete even though we were smugly pleased at our own results at tilling the land.

Despite many jokes about the postman only bringing brown envelopes and bills, we are sure everyone looks forward to delivery of the post. Envelopes were sometimes addressed to us 'Amy and Heather' Brandyburn Cottage, Ballyconneely, Co. Galway, and on one occasion, only our names and County Galway. Surely some local person worked in the Sorting Office in Galway city for letters arrived safely. Galway is a quite sizeable County, in fact the second largest in Ireland after County Cork.

During one of our many attempts to lose weight, the fact had been mentioned in a letter to a friend in Yorkshire. She had a tremendous sense of fun and addressed her next letter to 'The Two Sylphs', Brandyburn, etc. Postie looked strangely at us as he asked, 'Is this for you?' He came to realise that our friends were as eccentric as we were, for that particular friend used many descriptions sometimes flattering, others with a wicked turn of phrase, but John was always courteous and faintly amused that the 'ladies of Brandyburn' got such unusual envelopes.

We told our friends in the sitting room of another example of 'being known' when guests who had visited us, having gone south to Killarney afterwards, met up with a couple from Northern Ireland and, extolling the merits of Brandyburn Cottage, recommended them to visit us on some future occasion. A year later the time came when the couple decided to make a reservation. 'What was that name we were given?' they queried each other. Well, it was a Guest House in Roundstone they thought, run by two Scotswomen. So phoning Roundstone Post Office with their query they were directed to Ballyconneely Post Office where Mrs. McWilliam, our Postmistress, told them, 'Yes, you are looking for Brandyburn Cottage in Ballyconneely and the ladies are Scots'.

'Please put us through', the prospective guests requested.

The caller being told there was no reply from Brandyburn said, 'But there must be - it's a Guest House'.

Mrs. McWilliam agreed it was a Guest House, but told him, 'It is a lovely day here and as the two ladies are keen gardeners they will be out of doors and not hear the telephone bell. Would you try again after four o'clock?' which he did and a week later we welcomed them to Brandyburn.

Then an extraordinary coincidence occurred. We introduced them to the other two couples present in the dining room at dinner and, as usually happened, the conversation flowed. Later when we were all having coffee in the sitting room, it transpired that the three men had been in the same class at school about forty years before and this was the first time they had met since their school days. One lived in the north of Ireland, one in the midlands and the third in Dublin and they met again in the west of Ireland at Brandyburn Cottage.

THE LONG ARM OF COINCIDENCE

When we first arrived in Ballyconneely we discovered that the Community School in Clifden offered a good range of evening Adult Education Classes and opted for a class each. Amy went to Cookery Demonstrations by a top chef from Galway and enjoyed the evenings learning new ideas and meeting local ladies. Heather tried her hand at pottery - again. Her class was taken by a young man who explained that he was deputising for the teacher for two weeks. He introduced himself as Brendan and came round the class establishing how much or how little each student knew. When he came to Heather he asked if she had an idea what she would like to make. Her reply was, 'Yes, a dinner service or Ming vase'. The first was no idle challenge, the second was. She explained that she had attended a class in Dublin and had embarked on the goal of a dinner service but coming home by bus one night clutching three treasured soup bowls, the bus lurched and it was a case of the three bowls or Heather flying off the bus, so the bowls lost the decision. She now wanted to have a second shot at producing some more bowls. Her friends in Dublin, when told, groaned as they had all been recipients of her doubtful talent, but this time hoped she would perhaps 'get it right'.

As time went on, she didn't achieve much in the Clifden class either, but friendship blossomed with Sandy the 'real' teacher who owned the local successful pottery ; Marianne a Dutch weaver, who also had her own thriving business and was married to a Clifden man, and Brendan who was in his family's hotel business. Amy and Heather enjoyed the friendships which had emanated from the pottery class. The knowledge which Brendan and his family had of the area, both past and present, was extensive and the family's interests seemed boundless - gardening, music, theatre, history, crafts and folklore.

We have said that coincidence figures largely in our lives and when preparing colour slides for a talk to the Irish Countrywomen's Association Heather found a box of slides taken on her first ever trip to Connemara many years before, and began looking through them. She came upon one she had taken as a possible entry for a competition of a small boy standing in shallow water, holding a crab at arm's length. His face beamed with achievement under an unruly mop of curls. Handing the photograph viewer across to Amy, Heather asked her who it was. Immediately came the answer 'Brendan'. And it was indeed. Showing it to Brendan he could hardly believe the coincidence, but confirmed he was the wee boy guddling for crabs down the Beach Road at Clifden.

We have told you about the coincidence of our first paying guests and mentioned a sequel. Heather's friend Alice in Maryland and her sister Ruth were out driving and had to pull up behind a car at traffic lights in a small township in the Maryland countryside. The lights changed and the leading car moved off as did Ruth, but the first car stalled and Ruth gently rolled into the back of it. The two drivers got out to exchange the usual pleasantries, but as there was virtually no damage the atmosphere was very amicable. Alice had also got out of the car with her sister and as the two drivers exchanged names, she was surprised to hear the man say his name was 'League'. Immediately she asked if he came from such and such a township. Very surprised he nodded 'yes'. Whereupon Alice continued, 'Yes, and last year you stayed one night in Ireland at my friend's Guest House, Brandyburn Cottage in Ballyconneely'. Quite right. The Leagues were our very first paying guests, whose son had begged us to 'go easy on the greens'. Ballyconneely, Connemara, and a country town in Maryland USA - it is a small world and a big coincidence.

Friends of friends who live in Dublin popped in to see us each year when they spent a summer month in their caravan which was permanently parked overlooking Dog's Bay at Roundstone. They had initially stayed with us one night whilst making preparations for their Summer holiday and each subsequent year they booked themselves a dinner 'treat' with us. They were interesting people and knew a great deal about the seabirds and the nearby islands, their history and folklore.

One year, arriving for dinner, they told us they were very intrigued as each morning when they pulled back their curtains there was always the same car parked along the road overlooking the beach and the owners were out enjoying the sunshine in their lounger chairs. They seemed to have a routine of walking, reading, picnicking, etc. That evening when Seamus and Maura were having a pre-dinner drink, to their surprise who should walk into the sitting room but the mystery car couple. Being the only visitors in the sitting room at that moment they introduced themselves and by dinner time had decided to sit together and continue their conversation. For the rest of our guests' holiday they visited Seamus and Maura in their caravan each morning for coffee and homemade biscuits, after which they would stroll and chat, Seamus and Maura imparting their wealth of local knowledge.

Even such short friendships are a bonus to a good holiday.

MORE THAN GUEST HOUSING - THE TOURIST BIT

For many years County Galway was a favourite place we visited at every possible opportunity. We had experienced most of the weather vagaries ! But when actually living there permanently, we changed our whole attitude to the elements. Heather never did like winds and gales and even now still gets an unsettled feeling when strong winds and gales blow in from the North Sea at Hull.

In conversation with two Americans one day while driving the elevating Sky Road they said their greatest pleasure on this visit was the vastness of the skies, commenting that in their native New York views of sky were certainly so limited as to be non-existent, an opinion we shared after our visit there.

Our friend Pauline in Dublin had a hobby of making place mats. We were fortunate to have some sets with subjects such as 'Georgian Doors', 'Irish River Gods', local views and a range called the 'Skies of Ireland' graced our dining room tables. They were a real talking point. For these pictures were particularly colourful to the extent they were almost unbelievable.

We reckoned we had seen every one of them in reality - muted and vivid blues, greens, greys through brooding browns and the wonderful rainbows heralding sunshine through raindrops.

Many of our guests were not slow to recognise the opportunity to watch nature's technicolour marvel rather than television.

A tourist without a camera is exceptional. There is so much of interest to see, the big decision is what not to take. Sunsets are always a must to the amateur and at strategic points for the show there were almost traffic jams. The camera enthusiasts gathered in small groups discussing the technicalities of photography setting the various controls on the camera by which time the colours had changed and the camera had to be readjusted. Quick-on-the-draw technique was paramount in the clear air of the west.

Clifden, the capital of Connemara is a very busy tourist centre. In summer in addition to Irish and British touring coaches those from Europe are a common sight as are the many cars displaying a variety of European plates.

Quite a number of businesses have been started by non-Irish 'entrepreneurs' such as weaving, pottery, carpet making, fish farming, fish smoking, thatching and garden centres. All these enterprises have given employment in the area, the incoming families integrating into the community in all aspects and attending local schools and churches.

Clifden is likened to a Swiss village nestling at the foot of the hills facing on to an inland sea loch. Many years ago, the sea was the entry to Clifden for all its supplies which after landing were taken by horse and cart along the tracks to their destinations. There is very little commercial activity at the harbour now, a deep sea shark fishing business and the local inshore RNLI base providing most of the traffic. For the influx of visitors there are many Guest Houses, cafes and restaurants catering for all tastes. Likewise. first class hotels are either in Clifden or nearby, many of them internationally acclaimed.

A tweed mill produces colourful bales of high quality material and smart garments are to be found in the shop along with hand knitted and machine made garments. The Aran sweater is still much in demand, the hand knitted oiled wool garment being much sought after. Each sweater relates a story through its stitches, for families work their own patterns. Every stitch has a meaning, such as the cable - the fisherman's rope which denotes safety and good luck when fishing. The women who design and knit the sweaters are very skilled, chatting and knitting without looking at their work as it grows in their hands along with the regular clicking of the needles beating out the rhythm of a wild Irish jig.

Market Day in Clifden was an exciting, bustling happening. From early morning, cattle for sale were driven up the boreens and main roads to Clifden where they stood grouped in small invisible corrals awaiting sales. The market took place at the meeting of the road from Galway and the others which radiated as in the spokes of a wheel - north to Westport, south to Ballyconneely and Roundstone, Clifden Main Street going west where it further divided to form the way to the harbour, beach and sailing club and at the right fork the Sky Road climbed ever upward.

A circuit of Clifden often resulted in mutterings from visitors and locals alike, the old phrase 'a bull in a china shop', as they threaded their way on market day. Stallholders from outside came, hail, rain or shine, to set up stalls selling the typical street market goods.

One summer an enterprising teenager had a small caravan selling enormous pancakes with jammy fillings - an enticing waft of fruity smells encouraging the buyers.

Fruit and vegetables on the stalls shone on a summer day and dripped on a wet one, but still the buying and selling went on. An enthusiastic Garden Centre owner from near Galway came weekly and on market days encouraging interest by locals and an attraction for the visitor.

By the end of the 80's, a Cattle Mart had been built to conduct the business of sales. With so much documentation for licences and veterinary certificates it had become a necessity. Somehow the style of a handshake in an open street and the follow-up of a pint of Guinness to seal the bargain was lost in the new system of buying and selling beasts.

Entrepreneurial talents spring up in the most unexpected places. The first time we saw this particular talent was in a Clifden Hotel about eleven o'clock one morning. A very tall man wearing a large stetson and dressed ready for a day's hard horseback riding sat in a high-backed porter's chair, giving the impression that here was a man holding court. Occasionally young women came up to pay homage and were also dressed in riding gear with an accompanying abundance of gold jewellery. A small mountain of luggage rested nearby just waiting to erupt and scatter its leather and canvas in a wider area.

Being of a curious disposition and disliking loose ends we put this down to an eccentric group with an even more eccentric leader leaving the hotel and having a ride somewhere.

Later in the morning when we were passing Mannin Strand we witnessed what looked like a John Wayne movie. Our 'big man' of the hat, last seen sitting in state in the tall chair, was now astride a large handsome horse leading a charge of his followers. They were moving along that beach with all the urgency required on the large screen, but no gun fire, just pounding hooves.

Obviously a mystery to be solved, so …. put it on the Gerry list. We did get the answer. A young man from the Galway area had started an up-market pony-trekking business, taking groups on horse-back on a route covering different terrains. They stayed at first-class hotels and luggage was transported by mini-bus between the overnight stops. This proved to be a popular tour with Americans. It must be an exhilarating sensation to ride full tilt along the water's edge of the beach.

Once again, someone with an idea develops it into a tourist attraction and offers another aspect to the industry.

Two very important historical events which took place close to Clifden were the building of Marconi's shipping wireless station in 1907 and in 1919 the landing by the fliers Alcock and Brown within the perimeter of the Marconi Station. This had been the first non-stop transatlantic flight from America to Europe.

From Marconi's first experiments of wireless telegraphy in 1896, he had set up shipping wireless stations in West Cork, County Wexford and County Donegal and eventually in 1914 the Radio Station at Valentia Island in County Kerry. Clifden was the largest to be opened and was a busy early enterprise employing many people. Unfortunately during the Civil War it was attacked in the summer of 1922 to such an extent that it was never to operate again. It should be a matter of local pride that, in the early days of wireless telegraphy, Clifden played such an important part in Marconi's advancing knowledge for the world.

The bogland around the Marconi Station is strewn with the abundant rocks and boulders of the Connemara landscape, and it must be a near miracle that the small biplane piloted by Captain John Alcock and his navigator Lieutenant Arthur Brown was not smashed to pieces on the rocks. The bogland cushioned their landing after travelling nineteen hundred miles which took sixteen hours over the open sea with no chance of rescue if anything had gone wrong. To today's child a speed of one hundred and twenty miles per hour is that of a car and not a plane, but that brought the fliers across the Atlantic. It gives more meaning to the phrase long-haul flights.

On a nearby hill stands a monument to this historic event in 1919. It is built of limestone and represents the tail fin of a plane; an attached plaque notes all the details of the flight. Looking over towards the landing site, now marked by a large white cairn, the visitor must marvel at the courage of these two men who set out on this lonely journey and to finally find a safe landing place in such a remote area of the west of Ireland.

County Galway has an extensive road system. Many of the roads are built over bogland with the result that they are liable to create quite a bit of unevenness of road surface over a period of time. Often car drivers are frustrated by stretches of repairs involving a deep layer of road metal stones and feel they are making a first impression of flattening before the road roller takes over. When Clifden had mini pot holes, a wheel barrow was pushed along by a Council worker, the barrow containing small stones and a watering can of soft tar. The tar was poured in to the offending hole then filled up with the stones. This repair could be thwarted if a vehicle came along too soon, ran over the repair and the contents shot out.

A good example of this type of uneven surface road is the Bog Road which covers eight miles and is part of the cross country route between Clifden and Roundstone as we have mentioned before when our friends Joan and Doug once visited.

South of Roundstone a narrow bridge joins the Inishnee peninsula to the mainland. Quite a community lives on the 'island', locals and people with holiday homes. Many years ago the population had to cross to Roundstone by rowing boat to collect shopping, take children to school and go to Mass on Sunday. The bridge must have been greatly appreciated when it was first built for heavy goods such as building supplies were particularly difficult to transport before then.

Around this area it is fascinating to see the rough looking grey lichen clinging to the branches of the few trees and hawthorn bushes, proving the good air quality. Originally some of the lichen and other plants, such as roots of water lilies were used in the dyeing of wool and woven materials.

During the months of July and August, Regattas take place around the coast, including Roundstone. An exhausting programme of events is carefully planned, something to suit every taste. Talking of 'taste', it seems as though everyone eats seafood, and we wondered if something equivalent to 'jungle drums' took place in the depths of the sea, warning mussels, crabs, lobsters and prawns that it was that time of year again and so they should head for the underwater hills and hide.

Among the revelry there is a Regatta Dance , a real swinging affair and participants have to be in full health to cope with the pace. Five of our younger guests went along to the great Dance, the girls spending time in preparation of making a good impression. The party comprised a young married couple from Dublin, a German whose wife decided against going and two sisters from Dublin. They were all of an age and a warm friendship had developed between them.

The 'Hall' was packed and they squeezed in to join the gyrating, arm flaying dancers. As the advertising material had listed dances to suit everyone, eventually the pace changed and it was the moment for the waltz to come into its own. The floor had cleared a bit as thirsts had to be quenched. A tap on the shoulders of our two sisters introduced them to two local lads and they were swept off to the romance of the waltz. As it happened, they were almost literally swept off their feet by the two lotharios who were still wearing their welly boots, having come straight off their fishing boat ! Mercifully, the waltz was a short squeaky experience as the welly boots stuck to the floor and made smooth movement almost impossible. Beautifully mannered, the two young men assured their partners they would be back for another dance with them.

There are times in this life when we know enough is enough. The two sisters and their three friends from Brandyburn laughed together at their hopeless efforts to dance with their welly booted friends so they retreated to one of the local pubs then returned to Ballyconneely. The girls received a teasing which they took in good part as the story of the Dance was relayed to the rest of us. They had enjoyed their Regatta experience but agreed a ballroom of romance it was not.

North of Clifden on the road to Westport, there stands the magnificent Kylemore Abbey which is the monastic home of Benedictine nuns who came across from Belgium after the first World War. Kylemore is known world-wide as a boarding school for girls, also taking day pupils, and retains a very high reputation for its standard of education. The nuns have also put their business acumen to good use by successfully running a high quality craft shop and large cafe, both of which are extremely popular and an important venue on the Tourist Trail. In their pottery studio the nuns train potters in the art of their own distinctive designs which can be seen and enjoyed by the visitor. During the school's summer holiday period, it is possible to enter a part of the Abbey and visit the small chapel which is in daily use by the Order. In the grounds of the Abbey, close to the main road, stands a small Gothic church, reputed to be a replica of Norwich Cathedral in England.

In early summer, the area is a mass of colour from the wild mauve rhododendrons which are considered a weed and are very invasive. Even the brave hearts who sit in a boat on one of the Kylemore lakes hoping to catch a salmon - or even a tiddler - have a superb view to look at.

The mountain at the back of the Abbey is steep and rugged, but it is worth puffing up to visit the Sacred Heart Statue and taking time to contemplate a while. To gaze upon the peace of the lakes and hills must be good for the soul, even the patient fishermen on the loch must sometimes think of something other than fish.

The first time we drove up the Sky Road from Clifden we were astonished at the magnitude of such a panorama. We encouraged all our friends to take this road for a thrilling sight and explained that, although a single track road, there were adequate passing places. Travelling up the winding road, it is possible to look down towards the sea and catch a glimpse of Clifden Castle which was the mansion house built for John d'Arcy the founder of Clifden. In the style of a castle, it had an impressive driveway to take a coach and horses to the house which although now a ruin, the size of the rooms can clearly be seen. Hidden in the grounds are a grotto and shell house, both now in the same state of disrepair as the house.

Drivers find they cannot safely stop and view till reaching the summit car park. Arriving there the views are broad and absolutely stunning: Slyne Head lighthouse about nine miles distant : the sandy bays on the road from Clifden to Ballyconneely : a scattering of islands, some inhabited : just the enormity of it all, and again the peace on a calm, sunny day is unforgettable. Looking down into Clifden Bay you may be lucky enough to see the dolphins which have come in following fish. Folklore has it that this is a sign of good weather to come and we all like to believe that ! But even in days of the sea's anger when it rolls to the land in great heaving masses to crash on the rocks then rise as giant white stalagmites, who can be immune to such power and beauty ?

Reluctantly pulling away from this natural theatre, the twisting road continues on past white-washed cottages and winds its way down to the more placid shores of Streamstown Bay.

We loved this circular route so much we wanted all who stayed with us to experience it. Growing in reckless abandon along the road and hillside is the gorse or, as it is sometimes unkindly referred to, 'Ireland's gold'. The golden yellow flowers bathe the grey stoney landscape in vibrant colour and our two American friends from Ohio, Eleanor and Fritz, were greatly impressed by this artistic display. Fritz with his slightly Germanic intonation found it difficult to pronounce gorse. He always seemed to tongue-twist it to gross, and to this day in their letters Fritz and Eleanor always repeat the good-natured teasing, 'Is the gross still blooming ?'

Continuing on the main road towards Kylemore, passing through Letterfrack, is Tullycross an interesting and very popular centre for tourists to sample the successful rental scheme of Irish cottages. They do have thatched roofs and roses round the door, but inside all mod cons make life very comfortable for the visitor. It is an excellent centre for walking, particularly along sandy beaches. Beach-combing is a happy pastime and many a child's bucket goes home after the holidays full of shells and pebbles.

From Tullycross we enjoyed going towards Renvyle village and further on to the road which took us up to the foot of Tully mountain. This was another extremely narrow undulating road which required concentration. It was not for the faint-hearted driver as it gradually snaked its way up and along the mountain, finally dropping down towards the little fishing harbour of Derryinver.

Passing Kylemore the route takes the traveller on to Westport. By travelling west along Clew Bay, with the Holy mountain of Croagh Patrick forming an impressive backcloth, this forms a circular tour passing through Louisburgh and coming along the shores of Doo Lough to Delphi which appears like a small oasis of trees in a vast treeless landscape. Some of the finest mountains in Connemara surround Delphi, Mweelrea of nearly two thousand eight hundred feet being the highest. A continuation of this route works its way along the side of Killary Harbour and back to Leenane.

Instead of travelling on to Westport, another circular tour offers itself after leaving the main road at Kylemore and branching down through the Inagh Valley to Recess. This is yet another lonely valley of great beauty. To complete this circuit the road by coast through Cashel and around Bertraghboy Bay to Roundstone displays a different terrain, equally interesting and beautiful.

Although many of Ireland's lakes and rivers are free to fish, some require licences to indulge in this sport. Certain privately owned rivers, such as Ballinahinch, require a licence for a day's fishing, but a good day's sport can be had without this expense. The world's problems seem to melt away in silent contemplation, as long as there is a rod in the hand, standing in the water or sitting in a boat.

Before this chapter begins to sound like a heavy book on Visitors' Tours around Connemara, we make no apology for wanting to tell you of our delight at all this grandeur and beauty practically on our doorstep. Indeed our enthusiasm caused some of our first-time guests to ask us at breakfast, 'Right then, where should we go today ?'

Our 'conversations' in the sitting room must have encouraged their explorations.

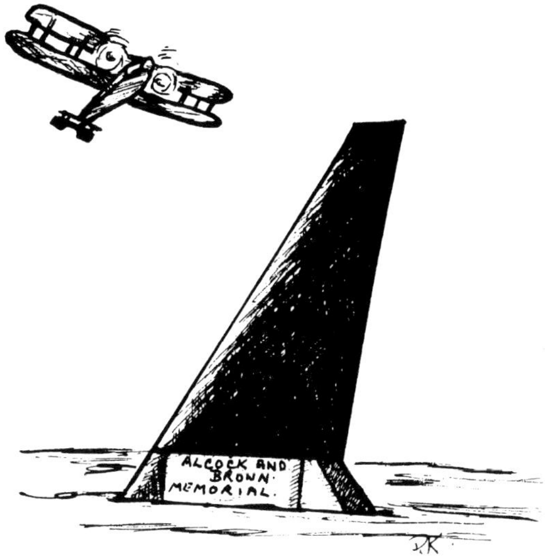
ALCOCK AND
BROWN
MEMORIAL.

THE SCHOOL AROUND THE CORNER

We were always delighted to invite our personal friends to visit us outwith the tourist season which roughly was from Easter to September. We had time then to take them on drives to our favourite places and extol the marvellous wonders of Connemara.

We had asked Margaret from Paisley, Scotland, and her nine year old grandson for a visit. Paisley which is not a city, but is the largest town in Scotland, was a big contrast to the open countryside which Scott was experiencing for the first time. A little bit diffident at first he learned to join the other children in our neighbourhood and his new found freedom meant that he was like a frolicking puppy, charging over the bogs, disregarding his spick and span holiday clothes and coming for meals mucky from head to toe and squealing with delight, 'I fell into the bog, Gran'.

At bedtime he would tell us of the talk between the local children and himself and how 'things are so different here'. We asked if he would like to go to school with the children for a half day and he was excited at the prospect. We telephoned Mr. Kennelly, the Master of Bunowen School and explained the situation. 'Yes, I'd be delighted to have Scott for the forenoon', he replied.

We knew that there were only two classrooms and the Master's had an open fire which was supplied with sticks and logs which the children gathered. The other classroom had no heating, both having the wooden desks which had fixed seats attached to accommodate two pupils side by side. First thing before lessons started, one child in each classroom would sweep the floor. There were no school cleaners as in cities and towns but mothers on a rota did 'Spring cleaning' periodically, fathers taking on carpentry or building maintenance when required. When we told guests of the little school they were impressed that so much community spirit was evident.

It was a big contrast to Scott's school in Paisley. The Master had pinned up a map of the British Isles so that the children could see where Scott came from. Encouraged by the Master, Scott told of the size of his school with a lot of classrooms and many teachers for over five hundred pupils. He explained how all the children in his class learned their numbers, spelling and writing; how he played football on a hard concrete playground and sometimes fell and had skinned and bruised knees. For leisure activities Scott was learning karate and, on the Master's urging, demonstrated this 'art' on one or two of the boys in the class. Gran went along to the school to meet Scott who kept up a constant chattering about how different this wee school was to his bigger school in Paisley.

Bunowen School served the children down our road who lived more than a mile from Ballyconneely. Each teacher taught more than one grade but the children were in no way deprived by this method of teaching. It was necessary as there were insufficient numbers to warrant extra classes and extra teachers. The youngsters all had plenty of energy and participated in everything the education system put to them. Another school in Ballyconneely took the children from the surrounding area there.

After their years at the Primary Schools, they went to the Community School at Clifden. The School Bus serving the area south of Clifden collected the children at certain points along the way from Roundstone. Those from Inishnee had to leave very early in the morning, sometimes walking or cycling long distances to connect with the bus before it travelled nine miles to Ballyconneely and another three miles down our road to collect the children from Bunowen before heading back to the main road and on to Clifden. After school, this bus route was done in reverse order. Before their evening meal, many children had homework and chores to do, such as tending animals which is a never ending task. It certainly made it a long day for them, particularly in the depths of winter. It was a case of learning naturally from the parents and participating in the general tenor of life.

The Community School provides a wide and varied range of subjects and for one week in September they get the benefit from the Community Arts Week. New subjects are available whilst normal everyday school curriculum is put on hold for that week. This gives the children opportunity of attending Workshops on such subjects as Writing, Story Telling, Weaving, Computers, Pottery and outdoor sports, for example Canoeing, Rock Climbing, etc. Parents and interested local residents are welcome and encouraged by the school to participate and view the Exhibitions.

In the evenings local groups and solo instrumentalists perform at the school and at different venues in and around Clifden.

Although the students may not necessarily make a career in any of these subjects they have been exposed to, say, Screen Printing, it is another knowledge for them which they may come across again later in life in perhaps some distant part of the world. Learning a new subject or craft is never a waste of time.

All in all there is quite a Festival atmosphere in the air and indeed Arts Week has extended the tourist season as its reputation has become more widely recognised.

PALMISTRY - READING THE LOCAL MAP

Putting on one of our other hats, that of enthusiastic tourist information officers, we would suggest short trips within a ten mile radius of Brandyburn Cottage for morning strolls, afternoon lazing on the beach, or evening sunset gazing to marvel at nature's colourful palette. Friends and guests indicated their diffidence to try narrow roads and boreens which might mean difficult turning places or ending in someone's farm or backyard. Reassuring them by our suggestions they came back glowing with excitement as if they were intrepid explorers who had found new Continents ! 'We didn't realise the extent of peace and sheer beauty all on your doorstep', they would say. 'No wonder you left city life'.

Using Brandyburn as the left thumb of an upturned hand we suggested taking the first finger locally known as the Brown Road (we never did find out why it was so called). It leads through pastoral land, grazing ponies, bleating sheep, ending on a rocky shoreline alive with seabirds and herons awaiting the next meal.

One friend, Marjorie, who was visually impaired, always had a before-breakfast walk on the Brown Road revelling in the sounds and smells, and declaring that, for her, the Brown Road was close to Heaven.

The second finger of 'the hand' was a narrow road which we called Des's Road (need we say why?). Midway along its two mile length, a deep channel gouged the land on the left and when high tides overflowed, the road was impassable, happily only for a short time each day and night. Pity the people who didn't have a seafarer's knowledge and found themselves bedded down in seaweed! A bit like our experience we have mentioned with Amy's puncture at Aillebrack when we came face to face with a high tide.

Regaining what we say is the 'main' road from Ballyconneely passing Brandyburn and going west, under Doon Hill, is Bunowen Castle which is an imposing ruin, its castellated silhouette framed against the sky-line and a lovely backdrop to the lush green fields and grazing sheep in the foreground. The ruined chapel is at the sea's edge behind the Castle, not very accessible, and indeed safety of visitors to such ruins throughout Ireland is of great worry to owners of the land.

In a short while the pearly white sands of Bunowen beach tempt the paddlers and bathers into the blue sea sheltered by the harbour. Mind you, in stormy weather the seas send sand scudding up and over the road leading to the harbour. It was here we first met the Winklepicker who told us how and why winkles were so important to the economy. Local fishermen tend their lobster creels and land their fish catches at the harbour. The smell of seafresh fish, particularly when the smoking season is in full swing, gets the gastric juices going. We were fortunate to get our supplies from the fish factory run by John Roberts, our guests enjoying the freshness of the wild salmon, brill, turbot, plaice, sole, crabs appearing on our dinner table only hours after being caught, and twenty-four hours later for the general markets.

Lorna had a popular restaurant in her home in the hills above the golf course, a track leading prospective diners on their way. Arriving at a small lake which had to be skirted, and doubting ever arriving at Lorna's, a painted board at the next turn cheered them with, 'Keep going, you're nearly there', raising smiles and anticipation of the meal which awaited.

The fourth finger of our 'hand' leads along Aillebrack beach, passing cottages of local inhabitants and others owned by holiday-makers. One such cottage is of a friend, Mary from Oxford, who loved walking at low tide over on to Horse Island and on the nearby beaches collecting driftwood. Visiting Mary in her cottage, we vied with each other to put the large planks or logs, bleached by the sea on to the fire, seeing the fireworks of sparks leap up the chimney, all of four feet wide open to the sky. Mary had been coming to Connemara for many years. As she became older and arthritic, neighbours kept a watchful eye to ensure her safety on beach-combing forays.

Gerry O'Malley's garage is nearby and, though we had found it extremely difficult to find in our 'callow' days of 1980, it was surprising how many visitors had cause to thank Gerry and extol his workmanship. He came to the rescue of a few of our guests when they had difficulty with punctures or other problems with their cars. On one occasion he had to break into a car to retrieve keys which the owner had locked in. When purchasing the car, the owner had been assured that it was impenetrable and thiefproof - maybe all right in cities but a big problem in an isolated area without the expertise of a Gerry O'Malley to come to the rescue.

The Golf Course is a great asset to Connemara; a seaside links, treeless, testing conditions of wind, dry sandy fast running fairways and greens. It is with a great sense of exhilaration and achievement that the nineteenth hole is reached. The views all around are spectacular, tending to distract players as they gaze across to the Twelve Pins in the background and foregrounds of beaches, boglands and Errisbeg at Roundstone. Slyne Head lighthouse is nearby and features in Penny's poem on page 122 telling of Sean Crowley seeing it flashing as he made landfall at the Coral Strand.

Slyne Head lighthouse which was commissioned in 1835 has now been made automatic as almost all other lighthouses. Helicopters which were used to service the lighthouse with provisions, equipment and taking on and off the relief lighthouse keepers, are still used by service personnel for regular inspection of Slyne Head.

All around the Connemara coast, including Bunowen Bay, are the buildings of former coastguard stations. Some are derelict but others have been converted to dwelling houses or prestigous up-market holiday homes.

Presiding above the cliffs to the west is St. Caillin's Well, the place of pilgrimage at midnight in mid November with Masses being said in the open and parishioners from far and wide making the journey on foot, by horse, donkey, or bicycle.

The rocky shoreline took its toll of small ships and on one occasion a spectacular rescue took place which could only be explained by some supernatural force guiding shipwrecked sailors through the boiling surf and rocks to land safely, then to be guided up the cliff to drink at the Well and restore their strength. It is said that St. Caillin was the inspiration who overcame the abject despair and exhaustion of the near drowning men and to this day they, and St. Caillin, are remembered.

Continuing on the route of 'the hand', the little finger takes us to Doonloughan Village. When we say little, the road which meanders is all of three miles long. It passes a relatively flat expanse which once was used by the lighthouse keepers on recreation leave as a make-shift golf course. There are deep sand dunes leading to the sea and merging on to Mannin Bay and Beach, where the annual Summer Horse Races take place showing the expertise of local jockeys.

You must drive this road carefully watching out for roaming Connemara ponies who regard it as part of their 'range' and also to avoid some lengths of rubber piping laid alongside the land to convey much needed water, for not all the cottages and houses along here have connections to a water scheme.

Nearing the end of the road are the ruins of Doonloughan School which we were told had a roll of a hundred children at one time. They had to trudge over fields from Slyne Head, Bunowen and many 'townlands', as small villages are known. We wonder if they forgot the difficulty of getting to school and back as they enjoyed scampering about the shoreline guddling for crabs and shells. Their early environmental education was received in Nature's School!

Nowadays the children attend Bunowen Primary School and at the age of twelve move to the Community School at Clifden. Mostly the children outwith the three mile limit have to be 'bussed' to and fro.

Bunowen School was our local Polling Station which gave us the opportunity to see the classrooms with their old fashioned desks and inkwells such as we had when we were young.

Doonloughan was a favourite outing in Spring with its profusion of primroses. When Chris-Ann was in hospital in Galway she and the other women in the ward received posies of primroses which Heather had set up in small containers and placed on each bed table, thus bringing the lovely spring freshness to those countrywomen who were patients and away from their homes. The doctor commented that his ward had broken out in a yellow rash of primroses so he too was given a posy for his desk.

As you return along the road to Brandyburn the large ruined building on the left caused quite a lot of speculation by our guests. 'What happened there?' they would ask. This had been a seaweed processing factory employing many people but, as so often happens, economics made it impossible to compete with more modern technology. It was closed down adding to the already high rate of unemployment in the area.

Guests were always interested in the differences between urban and rural life and in the sitting room after dinner had many lively discussions. We were sometimes the object of fun as we told a captive audience of our naivety and downright ignorance relating some of the events we have already mentioned.

But one subject stimulated parents particularly and that was the future prospects of the local children when the time came to leave school. There was no industry as such to take significant numbers so some would cross to England or America while others got casual work on the land, the building and renovation of houses and, particularly in summer, the tourist scene when shops and hotels were busy. It is interesting to know that quite a number of local people did extremely well outwith Ireland : top administration in the Arts in London and serving on the staff of the Kennedy family in Boston being just two of such examples, but always they fervently supported their homeland.

We are sure one of Connemara's best ambassadors was Aine from Clifden in Bord Failte's Office in Paris. We were proud to be selected as a typical Guest House when Aine brought a party of French tourist staff on a familiarisation tour to see the facilities in Hotels and Guest Houses and to learn first hand of Ireland's tremendous potential for the visitor.

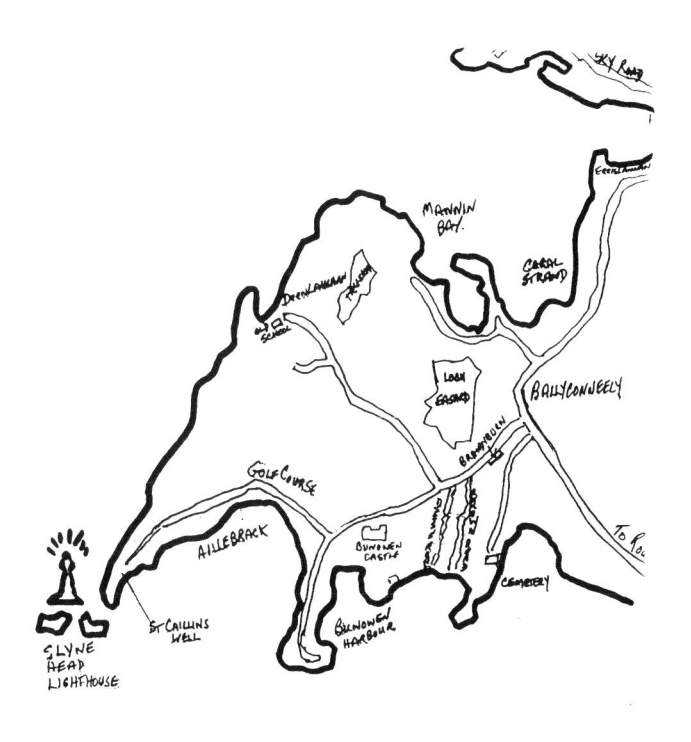

GETTING TO KNOW THE I.C.A.

As part of our forward planning before we left Dublin for Ballyconneely, we agreed we would try to become part of the local community, realising of course that we would be newcomers into an established way of life. We thought we would make an approach to the Ballyconneely Branch of the Irish Countrywomen's Association.

This Association has affiliates world-wide and on occasions Dublin has hosted International events. Our lunch hostess in Ohio had visited such a Conference, as we said, and had enjoyed meeting members from other countries, exchanging information about their own working participation at home.

The ICA had been formed to educate young women in isolated areas of the country on household management and farming skills. It was also intended to give them opportunity of meeting contemporaries on a social level as in remote districts there were few organised opportunities for women to meet.

The welcome we received was warm and sincere and dispelled any doubts we had of settling in. We enjoyed the programmes of social contact, handcrafts, talks on subjects of interest, and we like to think we were able to contribute to the success of these evenings. Group Meetings with branches at Clifden, Cleggan, Tullycross and Roundstone were held periodically, when we came to know more people and consequently this extended our appreciation of the tremendous work the women did in the home, on the farm and for the benefit of the schools, churches and local events.

When we first joined the ICA the venue for meetings was the local hall which had deteriorated badly over the years; the less said of its condition at that time the better. So when it came to the all-important tea interval one of the members had to stumble down the broken steps outside in the darkness and cross the road to the village pump some one hundred yards away. Filling the kettle she would retrace her steps and we, eagerly awaiting our cuppa, would have the old electric point switched on in the hope of boiling the kettle – sometimes it worked, other times ......Thankfully we soon moved to the excellent premises of Ballyconneely National School. In later years everyone rejoiced when as a result of fund-raising, work commenced on the renovation of the Community Hall, a tribute firstly to Father Seery, then Father Corrigan and the parishioners of the area.

During our first winter session of the ICA we were to assist with the Senior Citizens Party. Trying to gauge just how many sandwiches we should provide and asking for an approximate number of those who would come, a hazy answer didn't help. Nor did the starting time for the party. We were used to events starting by seven or eight o'clock, but were enlightened that all the old folks would first of all go to Keogh's pub until closing time when they would toddle over to the Hall. This was a good thing, for the socialising had started and the party in the Hall didn't need any 'ice breaking'.

The local musicians on tin whistle, fiddle, bodhran and spoons kept the feet tapping and accompanied the singers. The bodhran is an instrument which looks like an outsize tambourine, held by a cross-bar at the back. The supper as always was enjoyed and adequate liquid refreshment ensured.

These get-togethers were eagerly looked forward to by everyone. Celebrations of Christmas, St. Caillin's Day, St. John's Night and after Pony Shows and other events meant highlights against the normal daily round. In the ICA we were fortunate to have our own poet - Penny O'Malley. In her quiet way Penny would say, at our Christmas Dinner for example, 'I've a wee poem' and read it to us. At one of our celebrations in 1988 Penny recalled the landfall of a lone intrepid Transatlantic sailor who came ashore near the village.

THE LONE OARSMAN

His name it is Sean Crowley,
In England he was born,
He came of Irish parents
And one bright Summer morn,
He headed off for Canada
And brought his boat also,
From Halifax to Ireland
He said 'I'm going to row'.
His boat was 21 feet long
Made of fibre glass quite thin,
He wondered what he'd call her

And came up with 'FINN AGAIN'
So on the 17th of June in 1988
He stepped into his little boat
Not knowing what would be his fate.
After some weeks out from land
His hands were stiff and sore
His boat capsized five times one day
And then he lost an oar
The waves they washed right over him
He lost his camera too,
His craft she bounced like a little cork
As the storms around him blew.
For food on board he'd taken
Some sausages and beans,
Steak and raisins, nuts, and rice,
He had tea with all his meals,
If only he could shelter in a nice calm little cove,
For all he had to cook on,
Was a tiny wee gas stove.
For 97 days he rowed and sometimes slept and thought,
Of home, his family and friends,
And the worry to them he'd brought,
Then one night through the darkness
As he prepared for bed,
He saw a great big flashing beam,
T'was the lighthouse called Slyne Head.
One more day he had to row
When some fishermen he spied,
They asked him if he'd need a tow.
He smiled and then replied
'I've just rowed in from Canada',
So proudly did he boast.
Sean Crowley had just landed on the Connemara Coast.

Penny O'Malley
December 1988

    The cold and wet Sean Crowley was given wonderful hospitality at the Alcock & Brown Hotel in Clifden and presented the owner Mrs.

Ethel Keogh with one of the actual oars he had used. It had been mounted on the wall of the Restaurant where we were having dinner and Penny, as she read her poem, stood beneath that wooden oar which had seen so many miles of sea.

It was a pleasant experience to get dressed up for a night in the 'big city'. Not many of us would normally drive the sixty miles to Galway in an evening, so we hired a minibus to take us to a Fashion Show in aid of the Galway Hospice.

Learning of our sixty mile drive, the organisers had kindly reserved seats for us and we Oooooooh'd and Ahhhhh'd at the lovely fashions for all ages.

We had a marvellous time starting with a welcome glass of wine or soft drink at the Ardilaun Hotel, free samples of various cosmetics and participating in the Draw for excellent prizes given by businesses and organisations.

Evelyn's luck was in. She won a Microwave Oven! On the return journey all sorts of quips resounded as Evelyn was threatened that ICA's and neighbours would all drop in for a meal cooked in her Microwave. It was a fairly new piece of kitchen equipment at that time and none of us possessed one.

The inevitable stop for fish and chips increased the hilarity as we drove through the darkness ticking off the miles, and when someone spied a lonely cottage on a hill far away, its lights twinkling through the gloom, a chorus got up, 'Goodnight Bridie', or 'Mary Ann' or 'Finnoula' irrespective of whose cottage it was deemed to be!

Anyone who has travelled by minibus or coach with a group of women, be it twelve or fifty-two, has heard the noise level increase with each mile. We wonder what decibel levels are obtained but, no matter, women have the capacity for enjoyment of simple pleasures.

The ICA participated in the life of the Community to the benefit of so many people young and old. We all appreciated the co-operation of the Ballyconneely shops when it came to notices of meetings and events, and especially when we were mounting a display of the crafts we worked on at our meetings. The shops gave over a window to show a sample of the handwork - varied, colourful and deftly worked. There are many good pairs of hands to be seen working in rural areas and some of the unsung heroines could put machinery to shame.

Having said so, the menfolk have their own leisure activities, mostly involving serious talk of cattle, sheep and the world-renowned

Connemara pony, all usually accompanied by the delights of a 'jar' in the pubs. During July, each week there is a local Pony Show - Maam Cross, Ballyconneely, Roundstone, Claddaghduff and Cashel culminating in mid-August in the Clifden Show which attracts over four hundred entries.

The rugged environment has played its part in developing the Connemara pony which is hardy, intelligent, and has extraordinary jumping ability. To be registered as a Connemara Pony is not easy, for very strict regulations are in force to ensure its unique status is upheld. We enjoyed the annual inspection and registering of the ponies who were issued with their own special, Passports, the Inspector having his 'Surgery' at the centre of the village where pony and off-spring were taken to be vetted.

On Pony Show days the winners of the coveted rosettes proudly walked home from the distant Shows, stopping regularly for the owner to 'wet his whistle' in the pubs along the way. By the time the last few yards of the journey had been achieved it was a case of pony showing the owners the way home ! We never saw a lady owner following this routine and arriving home in merry state !

Signs to Ballyconneely Pony Show in July give directions to the Show Field which is on an elevated position above the village church and Community Hall. You can't help looking at the wider vista of the indented coastline nearby, a truly wonderful setting : blue sea, golden beaches, green swards and of course the Field itself is most inviting to man and beast.

Organising a Pony Show means lots of hard work, particularly for the men and women who will be competing, since these events sometimes include classes for sheep, cattle, donkeys and dogs. This is the format of the Ballyconneely Show and in order to keep the competitive spirit going, further classes are added such as fruit and vegetables, baking, jams and jellies, honey and crafted goods displaying knitting, embroidery, patchwork, rugmaking and crochet. The Hall is a hive of activity. The ICA ladies help in these latter classes and 'man the stalls'.

Children are not forgotten and a Painting Competition was inaugurated and opened to pupils from Bunowen, Ballyconneely, Roundstone, Clifden and Cleggan, the prizewinners being very proud of their achievements which were acknowledged by the Show Committee with the presentation of medals, cups and rosettes.

On Pony Show day the excitement mounts from early morning when the animals arrive, fodder and water supplies having been put in place. The parade ring is cordoned off and the loudspeaker van calls forward the various classes for judging.

Trophies and medals have been gifted by local people in recognition of happy anniversaries or indeed in memory of deceased loved ones. As the prizes are awarded, the citations show a tremendous sense of community spirit and the familiar Connemara family names are well in evidence.

In 1987 the Ballyconneely ICA celebrated its Tenth Birthday. At the Christmas Dinner Penny O'Malley read her contribution to the Birthday party. The following abbreviated version gives almost a potted history of the Guild and acknowledges her fellow members up to that time.

'I've been asked to write a wee poem.
I just didn't know what to say.
But now that I've started I'll finish -
It's all about our ICA.

The craft night it is all over
And it was a sight to behold,
With bedspreads and lampshades and bootees:
And cushions of green, white and gold.

There were rugs and rag dolls and crochet
There was knitting and patchwork too,
And a cockerel stood in a picture –
You'd swear he said cock-a-doodle doo.

And now it is our Tenth Birthday,
The Guild grew big this past year.
We had remained small for a long time
And must have been in the wrong gear.

Things are improving, Thank God, now,
We really have come a long way.
So come on, keep busy, continue the good work
And be proud of our own ICA.

When first we came to the meetings
The hall that we used was so cold –
No heat at all in the winter
With draughts through each curtain fold.

We'd plug in the kettle for tea-break.
We'd sit around and stories were told.
We'd go back to make the tea later,
To find kettle and water stone cold.

But things took a change for the better –
We moved from the Hall to the School
Cosy and warm altogether
In one lovely room as a rule.

We sit down and get our hands working
On cushions, rug making and tweed.
We are good little workers, content at our crafts.
A small push is all that we need.

There's Eileen, Helen and Yvonne.
There's Bernie and Kathleen and Joan.
My special thanks here are for Kathleen
For she always gives me a lift home.

There's Frances, and Ann and there's Annie.
They all come from Mannin together,
And those other two ladies who do so much work,
Of course, I mean Amy and Heather.

There are two Mary's, an Evelyn and Margaret
And Peggy is present also.
When it comes to making tweed pictures
Those ladies put on quite a show.

But there is one other person I've left out
I almost forgot her you see,
With all of this scribbling and writing
I nearly left out poor old me.

Goodnight to you all and God Bless you
I hope that for many a day
As Members we'll all be together
In Ballyconneely's fine ICA
That the years ahead will be happy
With everything turning out right.
Good Luck, Good Health, Merry Christmas
From me to you all now, Goodnight.

THE PARTING OF THE WAYS

Ten years in Brandyburn had given us great pleasure from the moment the idea was first talked about on Dun Laoghaire Pier and the plans started flowing. It was a memorable chapter in our lives. However when we first embarked on our enterprise in 1980 we kept in mind the fact that years have a habit of catching up on the unwary.

Taking stock was always a trait with us and realising we were getting older faced the fact : the time had come to do some more planning for the future - full retirement ?

Many things had to be considered. If we stayed on in the rural countryside and for example were without cars we would have to walk the mile to the village for shopping. Galway the nearest city was sixty miles distant. The bus came through Ballyconneely once a day in the summer months but only twice a week in winter. A journey of more than three hours each way meant an overnight stay in Galway.

If we were unfortunate enough to require hospitalisation in Galway, life for each of us would be extremely difficult to say the least.

To go further afield, for instance to visit friends in Dublin or the even longer journey to the U.K. would be taxing in time, effort and cost.

So, after much talking and weighing up the situation we agreed it was time to take full retirement, sell up in Connemara and probably it would be best to return to our roots.

During our years in Ireland, Heather's thirty-seven and Amy's twenty, we had made many friends and contacts. We were reluctant to leave but a new chapter was beckoning. Excitement was beginning to mount – a new life again. Amy had family in Scotland; Heather did not and facing the challenge took the view that the world was her oyster !

Property again. This time we were the sellers, going through the agonies of 'On again, off again' as potential buyers were caught up in the domino effect of frustrated sales of their own houses before they could buy. Eventually our sale was concluded. Brandyburn would continue in the same form, the new owners would stamp their character on it.

Contrasting our original removal of two households from Dublin to Ballyconneely we condensed our latest migration to a few pieces of furniture and thirty wine boxes each of personal china, glassware, linen, etc. were packed and transported to storage in Dublin to await further instructions.

The large number of wine boxes was not indicative of a tippling life style but we had gathered them so that we could eventually handle the packages more easily when we reached our new homes. We were already thinking of lowered muscle power in 'advancing years' !

In July 1991 at 3 p.m. we left Brandyburn Cottage. The cars, well packed with essential, more personal belongings, headed off in convoy en route Dublin, Larne, Stranraer. For Amy the next stop was Edinburgh while Heather still hadn't decided on her final destination. Never one to believe in going back to some place - perhaps because her family motto was 'Forward' - she stayed a few days in Ayrshire before heading south and east to Yorkshire.

The pioneering women had made separate decisions to 'pitch tent', this time without resorting to wall tapping and checking electric plugs.

To this day when we meet we relive our last hours in Ballyconneely. We had gone through all the rooms in Brandyburn Cottage with its memories of our ten years and finally closed the door in sad goodbye.

Before the two cars even reached Ballyconneely village, after a frantic flashing of headlights Heather stopped and came back to Amy's Fiesta. 'You won't believe this. I've left my handbag in the house,' said Amy with a nervous giggle.

We returned, peered in the kitchen window. Yes, there was the handbag sitting on the counter alongside the spare set of keys left for the new owner (the main keys were with the solicitors in Dublin).

By good luck the kitchen's upper part of split level door had small panes of window. Stealthily in case someone passed and saw two women lift a stone and smash a pane we broke in, retrieved the bag, sellotaped cardboard to cover the hole, and hared back to the two Fiestas.

A Good Samaritan was required. We knew exactly where to find him and arranged the glazing job. Shaking his head and enjoying the 'joke' he must have thought we hadn't changed much in ten years.

We set off once more, retracing our epic journey of 1980 still loving all Connemara had offered us in the past and would continue to love no matter where we were.

OVER AND BACK IN CONNEMARA - JUNE 1995

Rosie, Heather's Ford Fiesta, seemed to have wings in the heatwave as we travelled through England, Scotland and headed by Sealink Ferry from Stranraer to Larne. Through busy Belfast we edged our way, seeing again Harland & Wolff cranes, known as the Goliaths and, joining the spanking new road systems we reached Dublin.

For a few days we caught up with friends. After our almost obligatory coffee in Bewleys and a reunion with members of the Business and Professional Women's Clubs we walked Grafton Street joining the cosmopolitan throng and were entertained by numerous buskers.

The time came to leave Dublin and once again go west. We appreciated the great changes in the one hundred and fifty miles of roads to Galway city, a much smoother and quicker journey.

As we neared Galway the sky was ominously grey with heavy threatening clouds, but it didn't deter our walk-about of the familiar streets and we managed a browse in Kenny's bookshop. We emerged to find steady, drizzling, wetting rain. What was it our friends had said all those years before ? 'It always rains in the West'. But, as then, we were not downhearted and returned to the car, headed to the favourite hostelry in the city, though of course it was not the time of year for 'turkeys in baskets'.

We continued our journey west and passing through Oughterard which had been our first search for property we laughingly remembered our obsessions with wall tapping and 3-pin flat plugs.

With the incessant beat, beat of rain on the car roof we left Oughterard which we always regarded as the start of Real Connemara. Heading through the mist and rain (it was certainly more than a soft class of a day !) we reached Recess to see breaks in the clouds and the threads of glorious colour appeared as the rainbow arched over the land. As so often happens, the weather can change with dramatic speed and anticipation mounted as we continued towards Clifden, noticing developments such as a Heritage Centre and a new holiday village. Promising ourselves a visit to both, we pressed on to our destination, the hotel at Renvyle which had been the summer home of Oliver St. John Gogarty, the noted wit and writer-physician. The hotel displays a great wealth of his memorabilia.

Next morning the heat-wave conditions had returned and off we set for Clifden, wondering what changes we might find there. Everywhere prosperity was evident, freshly painted houses and shops, the latter tempting the throngs. Tearooms, restaurants and bars, catering for everyone's requirements, had increased in the four years since we had left.

Main Street had become part of a one-way system but congestion seemed to be much the same as we remembered. Market Street, being on a hill with cars parked nose to pavement on each side, still caused problems for touring coaches as they threaded their way to disgorge passengers. The service bus from Galway arrived adding to the fray as back-packers, and there must have been about forty of them, stumbled off to collect the huge packs at the luggage compartments. Food and drink, those essential commodities for this far flung town, have to come great distances so supply vans and beer lorries of different sizes all added to the volume of traffic, and the confusion ! Clifden was buzzing with activity.

Rediscovering the streets and lanes, we were given a real Irish Cead Mile Failte from the butcher, the baker, and the candle-stick maker, et al, as the cliche goes.

There was also the sobering sight of a funeral making its slow procession of respect round the town from the church, the mourners following on foot. Local shopkeepers lowered blinds and closed their doors as the cortege passed. Old traditions continue.

The tempo of life changed as we left the town to travel the route by Two Mile Bridge, Salt Lake, Ballinaboy Bay, noting again the Alcock & Brown Memorial on the skyline of Errislannan Peninsula. We passed alongside the fuschia hedges to the Coral Strand with memories of our picnic the day we first saw the cottage which was to become Brandyburn. Over the years many happy hours were spent bathing in the warm clear blue sea.

Here we were back in Ballyconneely.

We called at the Post Office to a warm welcome from post-mistress Mrs. McWilliam and daughter-in-law Cathie. Since we had left, the adjacent church grounds had been landscaped, the Statuary cleaned and re-sited. The church itself had been refurbished. The

Priest's new house had mellowed and sat very comfortably in the centre of the village. We recalled the old Rectory at the crossroads and Father Seery's efforts to get the rubbish dump removed from his doorstep.

Keogh's pub and supermarket were shining with a bright new colour scheme, and tourists were sitting at picnic tables enjoying their food and drink in the warm sunshine, making good use of Mrs. Keogh's now matured garden.

Shimmering against the soft blue-grey sky, the countryside was bathed in its heatwave, the sea sparkling with a million glittering diamond patterns as we made our way toward Bunowen. We glanced up at the water tank on the hill, remembering our 'Jack and Jill' experience of the hard winter.

Passing Brandyburn Cottage memories flooded back with a catch to our breath and we hoped the new owners were as happy as we had been.

Further along came change. Nestling under Doon Hill, a group of modern houses was being built and facing this project was a new stone cairn commemorating American fliers who had ditched off the west coast en route from Norfolk Virginia, to Iceland in September 1944. Half the air crew perished and the other half managed to reach shore after approximately thirty-three hours on a life raft. The survivors spent four days in Clifden Cottage Hospital where they were treated with care and compassion. This memorial was erected on the fiftieth anniversary in 1994 by the people of Ballyconneely and Clifden and also the War-plane Research Group of Ireland.

At the harbour we discovered yet another new building project of a small terrace of houses. With wonderful views from every window, we could imagine the owners waking up to the sounds of the seabirds and puttering of the fishing boats as they returned with their catches.

While the local population of Bunowen would be more than doubled during summer, we had the feeling that all these houses would be like so many other holiday homes, presenting a blank stare during winter months - no Christmas candles there to twinkle across the darkness.

Following the impression of 'our' peninsula being like a hand, we took the familiar roads to Aillebrack, Slyne Head, Connemara Golf Course, Doonloughan and then returned to Ballyconneely. We realised we would have needed very many more days to say 'Hello' to all we wanted to see.

On our last evening at Renvyle before heading home, as we strolled the beaches in the setting sun we recalled our decade in Connemara, our 'education' in rural life, our new friends, our visitors who became firm friends and who still keep in touch. We talked of the local changes which had taken place bringing prosperity and progress to many.

We thought of the part we had played during the ten years, hoping we had contributed something of ourselves to the community and perhaps we are still remembered in a good natured way as the two non-Irish, 'blow-in' seaside landladies.

It has been said that to return to places of special memories leads to disappointments. Not so, we go over and back to Connemara with joy and anticipation.